Thai
SELECT
AUTHENTIC THAI CUISINE
AWARDED BY MINISTRY OF COMMERCE
THAILAND

C000241762

DEP

Department of Export Promotion,
Ministry of Commerce, Royal Thai Government

www.thaitrade.com

TRADE WITH THAILAND BEGINS AT THE

Department of

The Department of Export Promotion (DEP), Ministry of Commerce, provides a comprehensive range of services for Thai exporters and international businessmen wishing to do business with Thailand. Acting as a one-stop service centre, it provides trade information and advisory services, match-making link ups, business networking, data on Thai products and manufacturers, as well as helping to find suitable trade partners.

Vision

The Department of Export Promotion (DEP), Ministry of Commerce, is a government agency responsible for promoting exports that earn foreign exchange and strengthen both the Thai economy and society, thereby, helping ensure greater economic stability. Our vision is to provide leadership in promoting exports that make a major contribution to the growth of the Thai economy.

Mission

As international trade, facilitated by modern technology, continues to evolve rapidly, relevant government agencies must constantly adjust their roles to keep pace. Responding to the export policies of the Thai government and those of the Ministry of Commerce, which is responsible for providing leadership in spurring both domestic and international trade, DEP has developed an efficient, responsive operation that stimulates the stable

Export Promotion

growth of exports through the private sector for the well-being of the Thai public.

One major role of DEP is to foster the development of the competitive capabilities of Thai companies and businesses by organizing activities and events that create opportunities to increase exports. DEP pursues a marketing strategy that helps Thai businesses reach their target groups by means of such activities as organizing trade shows in Thailand, participating in international trade fairs, organizing Thailand Exhibitions and Thailand Outlet events overseas, leading trade delegations and supporting joint promotions with foreign department stores.

DEP also has the additional and important role of explaining the philosophy of the sustainable economy to the private sector and how it applies to international trade. Based on the principles of moderation, sustainability, and common sense, it entails being knowledgeable, circumspect, and cautious in planning and in operations with constant regard for fairness to achieve balanced and secure responses to the rapid, wide-ranging changes in the economy, society, and the environment.

Every unit of DEP, encompassing headquarters and the five domestic regional offices, as well as almost 60 overseas offices, share the mission of achieving the export targets for Thai goods and services through effective co-ordination and prompt, efficient assistance in solving problems and overcoming obstacles to government agencies and to the private sector.

Thailand – The Kitchen of the World

Food is one of Thailand's important economic sectors, as it constitutes 14 percent of the country's total exports. It generates employment for 20 million people and provides markets for 80 percent of raw food materials from Thailand. According to the National Food Institute, good quality and safety standards are recognized as the strengths of the Thai food industry. Thailand has continued to promote food safety, aimed at contributing to good health among the people, and Thai food production and exports.

Healthy & Easy Thai Cooking

Thailand has been able to manage to use plant and animal species to meet its needs and for export. It is known as one of the few countries to have developed itself from an agrarian country to a relatively industrialized one, yet still maintain the importance of agriculture and food production. Today, the country has become one of the world's major food exporters.

The Government has a policy to promote Thailand as the 'Kitchen of the World' by encouraging the opening of more Thai restaurants overseas. The policy will also help promote exports of raw materials from Thailand for Thai food preparation.

Thai Food
IN THE WORLD MARKET

Thailand is one of the world's top rice producers, with an annual yield of 24 million tons.

Thailand is one of the largest exporters of sugar, tapioca, and pineapple.

Thailand produces and exports tropical fruits, which are well known throughout the world, such as longan, mangosteen, rambutan, durian, and longkong.

Thailand is one of the top ten producers and exporters of food in the world. Currently, Thailand exports to more than 100 varieties of food to over 100 countries and its agri-industrial sector earns over ten billion US dollars.

THAI RESTAURANTS AND
Thai Select

Thai cuisine appeals to consumers' palates around the world and has been ranked first in popularity among the four most popular cuisines. Moreover, Thai food is considered healthy, therefore, very much in line with the modern trend toward eating healthy foods. The Department of Export Promotion began promoting the Thai restaurant business in 1998 when there were about 5,000 restaurants worldwide, a figure that is estimated to have reached 12,000 in 2006. The target for 2008 is 20,000.

The strategy for achieving such expansion is twofold; for existing restaurants to open branches and for established brands to franchise. Critical to this strategy is improving operators' business skills in general and restaurant management skills in particular to ensure meeting the highest quality standards. In addition, good promotional campaigns and public relations will help ensure the increased and sustained popularity of Thai cuisine. The *Thai Select* programme with its seal that attests to a restaurant meeting official quality and hygiene standards provides assurance to consumers in the restaurant's service area, while also motivating Thai restaurant operators to maintain high standards.

In 2008, 1,095 Thai restaurants in 36 countries had qualified for the *Thai Select* seal and that number is expected to reach 1,200 in 2008.

WHAT IS "THAI SELECT"?

Thai Select certifies that the food, the hospitality and the atmosphere of the restaurant is authentic. Chefs must be carefully trained in the preparation and health benefits of Thai cuisine. Receiving this prestigious award isn't easy; the bar is set high and the guidelines are strict. Still, through training and inspections, high standard Thai restaurants worldwide have achieved this distinction.

So anywhere in your travels, look for the stamp of approval *Thai Select*. It assures you that delicious Thai cuisine is being served in a pleasant atmosphere, and with a famous Thai smile. It's not just a meal; it's a journey.

Objectives of **Thai Select** certification
- To increase the recognition of quality Thai restaurants.
- To recognize and endorse quality Thai restaurants.
- To encourage Thai restaurant owners to raise their quality standards to international levels.

Categories of Thai restaurants certified as a **Thai Select** restaurant
- **Traditional Thai Cuisine:** Restaurants offering Thai cuisine with traditional recipes and maintaining traditional Thai style.
- **Modern Thai Cuisine:** Restaurants offering Modern Thai cuisine incorporating food of different countries such as spaghetti served with Thai green curry sauce.
- **Special Thai Cuisine:** Restaurants offering specialty Thai cuisine.

Thai Select restaurant criteria
- The restaurant must provide areas such as dining facilities, kitchen, restroom, etc. according to Health and Safety requirements.
- The restaurant must employ an experienced Thai Head Chef or a chef with no less than one year's experience and training in preparing Thai cuisine.
- The restaurant must use an adequate proportion of Thai raw materials and equipment for preparation of Thai dishes.

Overseas Thai Restaurants in the Thai Select Programme 2008	
Country	Total restaurants
USA	405
UK	137
Germany	120
Japan	66
Australia	45
Singapore	40
Netherlands	36
France	33
China	23
Canada	19

Thai Cuisine

Thai food has rapidly grown in popularity among casual diners and gourmets alike, earning it a status as one of the world's most popular cuisines. And while most people think of spicy meals laced with chilli as the predominant factor in Thai food, this is far from the truth. In all Thai dishes, there must always be a balanced harmony of flavours. Few cuisines can offer such a wonderful array of sensations that will delight and tease your taste buds quite like Thai food. Whether in a rich or fragrant Thai curry, spicy soup, savoury salad, or sweet dessert, the competing and complementing flavours create a harmonious blend that once tasted will never be forgotten.

At the centre of every Thai meal is rice, the staple of the diet. Thailand is the world's top exporter of rice, the finest variety of which *Thai Hum Mali Rice* is widely recognized as the best in the world. While *Thai Hum Mali Rice* is the centre of every meal, herbs and spices are surely the heart of the meal. For it is these ingredients which provide the dazzling array of delicious and exotic tastes that makes Thai cuisine so distinct.

Thai Ingredients & Herbs

As with all cultures, Thai people have used herbs and spices for centuries as essential remedies and medicines. Is it any wonder then that Thai food is considered so healthy? What makes Thai food extra special is its intricate balance of spicy, sweet, sour and salty. The captivating aroma of *Tom Yum Kung*, a favourite Thai soup loved the world over, serves as a perfect testimony to the statement – a blend of flavours from fresh lemongrass, galangal and kaffir lime leaf.

Some of the herbs used in Thai cooking are common throughout the world – such as garlic, mint, onion, shallot and coriander. But more of them are exotic and, in the age of world fusion cuisine, some are known the world over and are even adopted for use in western cooking; for example lemongrass, Thai sweet basil, galangal, bird chilli and kaffir lime. But there are numerous other herbs that are important to many Thai dishes, but are mostly not known to foreigners. These include quite a number of wild green vegetables with extraordinarily strong aromas.

Garlic, shallot, onion, spring onion and coriander leaf and root are basic to most Thai dishes. They are the most-used herbs and, in a sense, form the foundation of Thai food. However, it is the more robustly flavourful lemongrass, galangal, kaffir lime, ginger, holy basil etc, that, used in combinations, define the unique flavours of individual Thai dishes. But there are other strong flavoured herbs and green vegetables such as lesser ginger (kra-chai), turmeric, ma-kaen, phak-phaew which contribute to the flavours of other regional and local dishes.

There is more to Thai food than *Tom Yum Kung*. It is the cultural heritage that contributes to so much variety. We get delicacies like *Pad Thai* from the north, a wide variety of curries from the south, grilled meats with *Som Tam* from the northeast.

Thai cuisine takes pride of place in its natural heritage, practised as an art form and handed down from generation to generation. Thai food not only tastes good but also looks beautiful, with intricate carvings and creative decorations. And a popular way to savour the delight of the Thai meal is dining together with a group of friends and sharing the many dishes together. It's always a hearty feast with fun and the fiery flavours of Thai culinary creations.

Thai Fruits

Thai fruits are well known worldwide for their fabulous taste and quality. Not only are they rich in vitamins and have a high nutritional value, they can be used as ingredients in various types of Thai recipes. In addition to bananas, mandarins, coconuts, mango, and watermelons, Thailand offers a wide range of fresh fruit that may not be as familiar. These include mangosteen, durian, longan, rambutan, and pomelo.

THAI TRADE CENTRE OFFICES IN EUROPE

AUSTRIA

Thai Trade Centre
Kopalgasse 47, A-1110
Vienna, AUSTRIA
Tel +431-748-5020
Fax +431-748-502012
Email
thaicommvienna@nextra.at

DENMARK

Thai Trade Centre
76 Hellerupvej 2900
Hellerup, Copenhagen
DENMARK
Tel +45-39626999
Fax +45 39626099
Email dep@thaicom.dk
Website www.thaicom.dk

FRANCE

Thai Trade Centre
8 Rue Greuze,
75116 Paris, FRANCE
Tel +33-1-56901212
Fax +33-1-56901213
Email thaitcparis@wanadoo.fr

GERMANY

Thai Trade Centre
Bethmannstrasse 58
60311 Frankfurt am Main
GERMANY
Tel +4969 2549464-0,
2549464-11,
2549464-12
Fax +4969 2549464-20
Email
thaitrade@depfrankfurt.de

Thai Trade Centre
Petzower Str. 1, 14109 Berlin,
GERMANY
Tel +49-30-8050040
Fax +49-30-80500451
Email thaicom.berlin@t-
online.de,
Thaitcberlin@depthai.go.th

ITALY

Thai Trade Centre
Viale Erminio Spalla 41,
00142 Rome, ITALY
Tel +39-06 503-0804-5
Fax +39-06 503-5225
Email thcomrm@flashnet.it,
thaitcrome@depthai.go.th

Thai Trade Centre
Via A. Albricci, 8
20122 Milano, ITALY
Tel +39-02 89011467
Fax +39-02 89011478
Email thailand@comm2000.it,
thaitcmilan@depthai.go.th

THE NETHERLANDS

Thai Trade Centre
Laan van Meerdervoort 51
2517 AE The Hague, THE
NETHERLANDS
Tel +31-70 3455444
Fax +31-70 3461005
Email comhague@euronet.nl

SPAIN

Thai Trade Centre
Embajada Real de Tailandia
Segre 29/2A, 28002 Madrid,
SPAIN
Tel +34-91 5630190, 563 0196
Fax +34-91 563 8090
Email
thaicom@ntserver.codeinf.com

UNITED KINGDOM

Thai Trade Centre
11 Hertford Street, Mayfair
London, W1J 7RN, UNITED
KINGDOM
Tel +44-20 74935749
Fax +44-20 74937416
Email
thaicomuk@dial.pipex.com,
thaitclondon@depthai.go.th

CZECH REPUBLIC

Thai Trade Centre
Holeckova 29
150 95 Praha 5, Smichov
Prague, CZECH REPUBLIC
Tel +420-2-57323030,
57325867, 57325882
Fax +420-2-57327555
Email thaicom@iol.cz,
thaitcprague@depthai.go.th

HUNGARY

Thai Trade Centre
Jozsefhegyi ut.28-30, No A/1
1025 Budapest, HUNGARY
Tel +36-1-2122738, 2251369
Fax +36-1-2122736
Email
thaicommbp@mail.datanet.hu

REPUBLIC OF POLAND

Thai Trade Centre
Warsaw Financial Centre
Building 9th Floor
ul. Emilii Plater 53, 00-113
Warsaw
Republic of POLAND
Tel +48-22 5407097,98,99
Fax +48-22 5407095
Email
info@ttcwarsaw.neostrada.pl

RUSSIAN FEDERATION

Thai Trade Centre
9, Bolshaya Spasskaya St.,
Moscow 129090, RUSSIAN
FEDERATION
Tel 001 007 -7495 9741501,
9741543
Fax 001 007 -7495 9741531
Email thaico@dol.ru,
thaica@caravan.ru,
thaitcmoscow@depthai.go.th

Healthy & Easy
Thai Cooking

Healthy & Easy Thai Cooking

This edition published in
the United Kingdom in 2008 by:
Evans Mitchell Books
The Old Forge, Forge Mews
16 Church Street
Rickmansworth
Hertfordshire WD3 1DH
United Kingdom

First published in Thailand in 2006:
Copyright © 2006 Amarin Printing and
Publishing Public Co. Ltd.
English Translation 2006
Nuengnuj Chaixanien

British Library Cataloguing in Publication Data.
A CIP record of this book is available
on request from the British Library.

ISBN: 978-1-901268-43-0

Printed in Thailand

Preface

Thai food is universally popular due to its tasty combination of sweet, sour and saltiness, appetizingly enhanced by the tanginess from an assortment of chillies used in typical dishes. This flavourful blend which has become characteristic of traditional Thai food remains distinctive in local fare until the present day.

Other ingredients that are essential in Thai cooking are spices and herbs, which, beside their aromatic quality, are known to have diverse health benefits. For instance, *Tom Yum* (Thai spicy hot and sour clear soup), a well known local specialty, contains galangal, lemongrass and kaffir lime leaves which can reduce gas in the stomach and help relieve dizziness and indigestion. The essence of many types of herbs can aid in regularizing the circulatory system of the body. The knowledge of using herbs in Thai cooking, derived from traditional Thai medicine, makes Thai food a healthy choice in a real sense.

With these unique qualities in mind, many popular recipes have been selected and assembled in this book and adapted accordingly to suit our modern day living. The techniques are given in detail and easy to follow. Further accompanied by colourful photographs, these compilations of recipes are suitable for those who want to prepare a hearty home cooked meal of tasty and nutritious Thai food, whether for themselves and their family, gracious entertaining, or simply everyday delight.

Contents

The Traditional Thai Way of Eating

The culture of eating in Thailand has been cultivated and developed over a long period of time. In the olden days it was often said that Thailand was the cradle for rice and water, there always being fish in the water and rice in the paddy fields. Even now, the Kingdom remains abundantly rich in plants and cereals, allowing everyone to prepare and cook food to satisfy their own tastes.

Since olden times, Thais have cooked with locally grown herbs to maintain a healthy diet and in this health-conscious time this has undoubtedly played a large part in increasing the popularity of this diverse, tasty, aromatic and colourful cuisine throughout the world.

Food for Festivities and Ceremonies in Thailand

As with all social developments the Thai way of eating has changed over time, however it retains its original roots and is a reflection of the cultures and lifestyles of past generations.

A part of that culture is to prepare special dishes to celebrate the many festivals and ceremonies held throughout the year. An example would be food prepared for a wedding, which would very often include Chinese

rice flour vermicelli *(Kanom ken)* which denotes long life together or, as an old saying has it, "To live together until holding a golden-topped walking cane and a diamond-topped club".

Some desserts served on auspicious occasions came about as a result of international trade with other countries which resulted in the importation of other produce and cultures, for example *Tong Yib* (Golden Flower) and *Foy Tong* (Golden Shreds), both of which have foreign origins.

Different Kinds of Thai Food

In general terms, Thai food can be classified into three categories: Traditional, Adapted and Modern.

Traditional Thai Food

This is the basis of Thai cooking; meals that have been prepared and served from ancient times, using ingredients found locally and being fairly easy to prepare. Such meals might include a spicy mixed vegetable soup and boiled vegetables served with a coconut-based dip. The desserts would be made from flour, sugar and coconut milk and served with a seasonal fruit.

Adapted Thai Food

This category is food which has been strongly influenced by foreign cuisines but has been adapted to local tastes and local methods and is now considered to be Thai food. Dishes such as *Kang Kari Kai* (yellow chicken curry) and *Mus-sa-man Kai* (red chicken curry) are by-products of Indian curries, while the numerous clear soups have their origins in Chinese cuisine. And many recipes for desserts such as *Tong Yod* (golden egg drops), *Foy Tong* (golden shreds) and *Sangkaya* (coconut custard) came about through trade with European nations during the Ayutthaya era.

Modern Thai Food

In order to cater to the modern trend for convenience and concerns about healthy diets, the more traditional Thai recipes have incorporated many new herbs and foreign ingredients, such as macaroni and other pastas. The results have been dishes which, while being difference in appearance to the more traditional dishes, have retained the original tastes and aromas and proved very popular with the Thai people, particularly so the young.

Northern Region

The food of the Northerners comprises steamed sticky rice eaten with chilli dips such as Green Northern Chilli Dip *(Nam Prik Noom)* and Red Chilli and Tomato Dip *(Nam Prik Ong)* or a specialized Northern Curry known as *Kang Hung Le*. Other local fares include fermented pork or *Naem*, Northern Spicy Sausage, Pork Crackling, and vegetables. The Northerners prefer food with mild taste and not particularly salty. The region being some distance from the coast, seafood tends to be expensive so is seldom a part of the everyday menu.

of boiled salted eggs and sweet pork. It is also common to find dishes from other regions on the Central region menu. Steamed rice is always served with 4 or 5 main dishes depending on the size of the family.

North-Eastern Region (The "E-san" Region)

Like the people in the Northern region, the North-Easterners eat sticky rice. They prefer food with strong taste and do not have particular taste for sour and sweet food. E-san food is mostly grilled or broiled rather than fried. They eat a lot of food which can be readily and easily caught such as frogs, red ants, and a variety of other insects, together with pork, beef and locally raised chicken. Seafood is seldom eaten as the region is not on the coast.

Southern Region

The flavours of the food in the South are hotter, saltier and spicier than those of other regions. The well-known dishes are *Kang Tai Pla, Kang Lueng, Nam Boodoo* or fermented fish sauce. The Southern people enjoy eating *Nam Boodoo* mixed with rice and plenty of vegetables, this dish being called *Kao Yum*. As a large part of the population of this region are fishermen, seafood is abundantly available. The vegetables that are typically found on the Southern menu are *Sato* and *Luk Niang*.

Thai Food, Not as Complicated as You Thought

Thai Food for home cooking may be perceived to be too complicated for amateur cooks both in terms of ingredients and method of preparation. For instance, to derive the coconut milk used in red and

The Central Region

The people in this region have a flavour for a milder taste with a touch of sweet. The cooking method is rather complicated and a lot of effort is put into making those delectable dishes. An example of such dish is a dip called *Nam Prik Long Rua*, an ordinary fish paste dip which is carefully arranged with accompaniments green curries, the husk and the shell have to be first removed, followed by scraping and shredding the flesh and squeezing the milk. However, for the modern-day kitchen, ready-made coconut milk is commonly available in the supermarket. As these instant products can also be stored for an extended period of time, Thai cooking is now deemed much more convenient, practical, and obviously less time-consuming. Curry paste, one of the main ingredients in Thai cooking, also has many components and the process of making is long and complicated. In former days, part of the process was pounding ingredients into a fine paste using a mortar. However, electric grinders and food processors are now available and make preparation easier and, for cooks with even less time, ready made curry pastes are available at all supermarkets as yet another alternative. Furthermore, these products are exported abroad and thus widely available outside Thailand.

Some manufacturers have also produced ready-made curries for export such as Red, Green and Mussaman curries. These instant foods can be conveniently heated with extra fresh meat and vegetable added, if desired. With modern technology, it can be seen that Thai cooking is not necessarily as complicated or time consuming as it is often thought to be.

Seasoning in Thai Food

Thai food usually is very tasty. Aside from the main ingredients used in Thai cooking, whether meat or vegetables, seasonings also play an important role to enhance the flavouring. Thus, one should keep in mind and become familiarized with all the key flavours prevalent in Thai cooking as described below.

Sweetness

The sweet taste found in Thai food is partly derived naturally from some of the various meats used and partly by adding other sweeteners to further enhance the flavour. The key sweetening agent is, of course, sugar, which comes in a variety of forms, including refined sugar, palm sugar, and brown sugar. As different kinds of sugars have varying levels of sweetness, the type of sugar used affects the overall flavour of food.

Refined sugar has a sharp sweetness and does not change the colour of the food. Palm sugar, on the other hand, is less sweet and suitable for food containing coconut milk. When dissolved over heat and added to Thai noodle dishes or even the Thai spicy casserole "Palo", palm sugar can improve the flavour as well as enhance the aroma. Brown sugar, in powdered form, is suitable for certain kinds of foods. Palm sugar cakes, made from boiling palm sugar, dividing into pieces and leaving to dry, can be stored for future use.

Palm sugar in soft cakes — Brown sugar — Granulated sugar — Pound cane sugar — Cane sugar — Palm sugar

Saltiness

The saltiness in Thai food is derived from fish sauce and salt. Fish sauce is added to main dishes not only for the salty taste but also for its unique aroma. Besides fish sauce and salt, soy bean sauce and other all purpose sauces are now used in Thai cooking, depending on the dishes made or the preference of the cook.

Sourness

Most of the sourness comes from adding lime juice, tamarind juice, kaffir lime juice, or vinegar. The acid agents used in seasonings must be carefully chosen to compliment each dish. For instance, when making salad, lime juice should be used for its aroma. Tamarind juice has a sweet and sour taste, suitable for mixing with food containing palm sugar as a sweetener, in order to enrich the flavour of such dishes. Kaffir lime juice is used in certain dishes that require its aroma. When mixed with lime juice and used in hot and sour vegetable soup, it will greatly improve the flavour.

Shrimp paste

Lime juice

Kaffir lime juice

Oyster sauce/All-Purpose sauce

Fish sauce

Tamarind concentrate

Coconut Milk Used in Thai Food

Coconut milk is one of the essential ingredients used in Thai cooking, especially in various kinds of curries. The sweetness in coconut milk gives the blend of nutty and sweet flavours. Coconut milk is one kind of fatty substance which is derived from the process of removing the husk and the shell from matured coconut.

The flesh is grated by hand or passed through a grating machine to produce finely shredded coconut from which the milk is squeezed, while adding a small amount of plain water. The liquid extracted from the coconut flesh should be white and milky and is suitable for making many kinds of food. However, coconut milk can be divided into two categories suitable for different kinds of cooking.

Coconut Milk from Unskinned Grated Coconut (Coconut Milk for Curry making)

The coconut milk used for making curry or many other Thai main dishes is usually extracted from grated coconut from which the dark brown skin has not been removed. The milk obtained from this unskinned kind of grated coconut is creamy in colour, rather than milky white. This kind of coconut milk is therefore not suitable for dishes that require a whitish appearance and is mainly used in making curry. Ingredients making up curry pastes give colour to the curry such that the creamy colour characteristic of this type of coconut milk will not affect the dishes.

Coconut Milk from White Grated Coconut (Skinned coconut)

Coconut milk is an essential ingredient contained in most Thai desserts. Therefore, the coconut milk used must be very white to give a more appealing colour to the dessert. The dark brown skin of the coconut must be removed before grating, so that the grated coconut will yield a pure white and delectable looking milk after being squeezed. However, skinned coconut milk is equally creamy and aromatic as is the milk from unskinned coconut.

Ready-made coconut milk are readily available today, contained in bags, cartons, cans, and other packaging. It can be commonly found in the supermarket or any convenience store, thus making cooking a more convenient. Moreover, any unused portion may be stored for future use.

Skinned coconut   Coconut for Curry making

Rice and the Thai People

In earlier times, Thais and other Asians used to eat wild rice, whenever it was in season. When it was unavailable, taro and potato were often eaten in its place. However, as the population grew, it was discovered how to cultivate and store rice and it became the staple diet for Asian people. As it became more plentiful, Thais used it to barter for other necessities, such as clothes, medicine and other food items but they did not believe in selling it because of the traditional belief that it was the soul of Mae Posop, the Goddess of Rice, who bestows both good and evil on mankind. Today, rice has become Thailand's main export, supplying to countries that are unable to grow it, due to their geographical characteristics and climate.

Rice is the staple diet of Asian people. There are different kinds of grain such as rice, glutinous or sticky rice, maize and wheat. In Thailand, rice is placed second in the main dietary groups, producing carbohydrate as energy for the body. Rice also contains many vitamins and minerals. Most Thai people eat rice, both plain and glutinous rice daily. Northerners and Northeasterners prefer glutinous over plain rice. This habit of eating is in accordance to customs and culture that have been passed on from generation to generation.

Rice grains have to be refined to discard the husks first. This process of refining produces wheat germ and bran, both very good for health. The unrefined or brown rice still retain many vitamins which are beneficial to the health. In the old days, rice grains were pounded in large mortars, allowing vitamins to be retained as opposed to most vitamins being destroyed when refining rice in present day rice mills. Most Thai people now prefer to eat white rice although it is less nutritious due to the loss of the wheat germ and bran. Though unprocessed rice contains seven to twelve percent of protein, approximately thirty percent of it is lost once it is processed. Thus, the body benefits less from daily intake of white rice versus unprocessed brown rice. White rice lovers forgo many minerals present in brown rice including:

- Vitamin B1 which prevents beriberi.
- Vitamin B2 which is used as a treatment for dry lips, inflammation of the lips, exhaustion, loss of appetite and photophobia.
- Phosphorus which helps in the development of bones and teeth.
- Calcium which reduces cramps.
- Copper which helps build blood cells.
- Iron which prevents anemia and help build blood cells.
- Protein which helps repair the wear and tear of the body.

However, since protein in rice is not complete by itself, it should be consumed with dried seeds in cereals to obtain the maximum benefit.

Steps to Cooking Rice

Traditionally, rice is cooked in boiling water. When nearly ready, the remaining water is then poured away and the rice is left to cook on low heat until soft and fluffy. The downside to this method is that minerals are lost with the discarded water. Thus, a new method of cooking rice similar to steaming was later developed.

With this new method, rice grains are first sorted to filter out foreign particles and then washed twice before placing into the cooking pot. Water should be 1.5 to 1 in proportion to the amount of rice used and steamed until the rice is fully cooked. Cooking time depends on the size of the pot and quantity of rice. Most of the nutritious minerals are retained with this method of cooking, which is similar to using an electric rice cooker.

There are generally two kinds of rice that Thai people are accustomed to, namely Fragrant Mali Rice and unprocessed rice. The method of cooking these two types of rice also differs.

Cooking Fragrant Mali Rice

As there is less fibre in Fragrant Mali rice than in unprocessed rice, less water is required for cooking. Tiny particles of dust and other grains are first sorted from the rice grains after which the rice is washed twice. Water is then added proportionately to the quantity of rice (1.5 to 1) and cooked in the electric rice cooker until soft and fragrant.

Cooking Unprocessed Rice

Unprocessed rice is more nutritious than processed white rice. The method of cooking is the same as with the Fragrant Mali rice, except more water is added due to its richness in fibre. The proportion of water to rice is 2 to 1 and cooked in an electric rice cooker until soft.

Noodles

History of Noodles

Noodles were first introduced into Thailand during the reign of King Narai, at which time Thailand had begun to trade with many foreign countries. Noodles appeared in Thailand when Chinese merchants brought them for their own consumption. They boiled noodles with soup and vegetables, and Thais also developed a taste for this while coming up with various local recipes using noodles.

The Chinese also brought along the method of making noodles by using rice flour and noodles and this became widely known among Thai people ever since.

Fresh sheet rice noodles | Small rice noodles

Chinese rice-flour vermicelli

Chandhaburi rice noodles   Glass vermicelli   Rice vermicelli

Following the Ayutthaya period, the population grew further, with more Chinese coming to trade and settle in Thailand. The Thonburi period, as a result, saw an increase in noodle-making. Noodles could be bought easily both on the street and from canal boats. They can be eaten with or without soup and such is how noodles came to be included in Thai food. Methods of cooking and recipes for noodle dishes have been adapted to suit the Thai palate and acquire its special characteristic up to now.

Noodles were previously produced only in Chinese families. The method of making noodles is first to soak rice grain overnight, which is then ground into flour. A large boiling pot filled with water is prepared with the top covered with a thin piece of cloth. As the cloth is wrapped over the pot, a small hole is left to allow steam to escape. A thin layer of flour is then spread over the cloth and covered with a lid while the water is boiled. A wooden spatula can be used to remove the cooked flour when ready. It is left to cool and dried off. In the process, cooking oil is used to smear on each layer while stacking. The finished flour is then cut into strips of desired widths and finally served in clear soup or stir-fried with meat and vegetables.

Vegetables in Thai Kitchen

Our bodies require a daily intake of groups of food. Each category has its own nutritious value and is beneficial to health differently. For example, vegetables not only are filling but are also full of food substances.

There are vitamins and minerals in vegetables which act as antioxidants. They contain fibre which helps and prevents constipation and intestinal cancer.

The vegetables used in Thai food are chosen to suit each dish and according to what are available in the market. Vegetables can be eaten either raw or cooked; be it stir-fried, boiled or steamed. Raw vegetables are used as accompaniments to spicy dips to lessen the hot taste of chillies. They are also mixed in salads, not only because of their nutritious value but also to enhance the taste of that special dish.

In the old days people used to carve hard-flesh vegetables such as papayas, pumpkins and cucumbers and make into serving dishes or used as garnishes. Nowadays these beautifully carved vegetables can only be found at festive functions. It is of utmost important to thoroughly clean the vegetables before use. They must also be pesticide-free to ensure good health and well being.

Medicinal Herbs in Thai Food

Herbs, plants and spices used in Thai cooking, not only add flavours and aromas, making this one of the most tasty cuisines, but also have medicinal properties which makes it one of the healthiest.

Kra-chai *(Fingerroot)*

It dispels gas and can help with digestion and colic. It treats discharges, regulates the bladder and fortifies the heart. It also contains many vitamins such as vitamin A, vitamin B2 and calcium.

Fingerroot is added to curries to enhance the aroma and to neutralize the strong odour of meat.

Ka-prow *(Holy Basil)*

It dispels gas, and helps relieve stomach pain and colic. It lessens nausea and vomiting beside inducing sweating. Holy Basil contains vitamin A, vitamin C, niacin, phosphorus, iron, calcium and betacarotene.

Holy Basil leaves are often used in curries and many stir-fried dishes. They can be used fresh or crisply fried and eaten as a condiment to the dish.

Ho-ra-pha *(Sweet Basil, Horapha)*

It helps with digestion and relieves abdominal pain, colic and indigestion. It contains vitamin A, vitamin B1, vitamin B2, vitamin C, calcium, iron, fibre, phosphorus and betacarotene.

Sweet Basil leaves are commonly added in both red and green coconut curries as well as some stir-fried dishes. In addition, they are consumed fresh as an accompaniment in many popular Northeastern dishes such as *Lab*, a spicy and sour minced cooked meat and *Nam Tok* or spicy and sour grilled meat. They are also eaten as boiled vegetable.

Bai-mang-luk *(Hoary Basil Leaf)*

It is used to dispel intestinal gas and is a helpful remedy for coughs. It also increases breast milk and acts as a remedy for some types of skin diseases. It can also act as a mild laxative and contains vitamin B2, vitamin C, calcium, iron and fibre.

The basil leaves can be served as an accompaniment for dishes using Chinese rice vermicelli or added to soups such as *Kaeng Liang*, a spicy mixed vegetable soup.

Hom-dang *(Shallot)*

It dispels gas, helps the bladder, regulates menstrual cycles, and is an effective treatment for the common cold. It not only helps with digestion but also promotes good appetite. Shallot contains selenium, which is a mineral that acts as an agent to enhance the working of enzymes between vitamin A, vitamin C and vitamin D.

Shallots are used in salads, *Lab* and various *Pla* a spicy meat dish with lime juice, fish sauce and Thai mint. They are also included in the ingredients for curry pastes. Somtimes finely cut and deep-fried until crisp, Shallots can be sprinkled on food for aromatic purpose.

Kra-tiam *(Garlic)*

It is known to lower high blood pressure, high cholesterol and blood-sugar. It can also boost the immune system of the body. Selenium, which is a mineral, and found in garlic, that acts as a agent to enhance the functioning of enzymes and interaction of vitamins A, C and E.

Garlic is generally used in all types of stir-fried dishes. Minced garlic is deep-fried until golden crisp brown and used for sprinkling on food for its rich aroma. It is also one of the ingredients used in making curry paste.

Sa-ra-nae *(Thai Mint)*

It helps relieve colic pain and distension of the abdomen. It also induces sweating and dispels gas. The leaves can be chewed to reduce bad breath and also to cleanse the stomach and intestines to reduce contractions. Thai mint contains vitamins A, B2 and C, as well as calcium and iron.

Mint leaves are used as garnishes in spicy dishes such as *Pla*, *Yum*, *Lab* and *Nam Tok*, which are salty and sour in taste.

Prik-thai-on (Green Peppercorn)

It helps with digestion and can relieve headaches and rheumatic pains. It can also be used to treat diarrhea. Calcium essential for strengthening of the teeth and bones are found in green peppercorn, which is also rich in phosphorus, iron, vitamin C, niacin, and beta-carotene.

Green peppercorn can also neutralize the strong odour of meat in curries or spicy fried dishes.

Kha (Galangal)

It is used to dispel intestinal gas and ease dysentery. Besides relieving the distensions of the abdomen, galangal also helps dispel phlegm. Galangal contains vitamins B1 and B2, calcium, fibre and phosphorus.

Galangal is used in various Thai soups such as *Tom Yum* or spicy hot and sour soup and *Tom Kha*, a soup similar to *Tom Yum* but containing coconut milk. Galangal is another ingredient also used in making curry pastes.

Ta-krai (Lemongrass)

Lemongrass has many healthy benefits. It helps with digestion, vomiting, lowering blood pressure and dispelling gas and is also used to treat fever, stomach pain, gallstones and other diseases of the urinary tract. It contains vitamin A, calcium, iron, fibre and phosphorus.

Lemon grass, is used in *Tom Yum* and various kinds of spicy salad with herbs such as *Pla*. Lemongrass is another ingredient used in making curry pastes.

Ma-krood (Kaffir Lime, Bergamot)

It helps dispel gas and relieves giddiness. Kaffir Lime juice is a remedy for scurvy. Bergamot leaves contain calcium, beta-carotene, and vitamins A, B2 and C.

Although Kaffir Lime can be used as a whole, only the rind or zest is used in the ingredients of curry pastes. The juice is used in those curries that require extra sourness and aroma, such as *Kanom Jeen Nam Prik*, a curry served with Chinese rice-flour vermicelli.

Khing *(Ginger)*

It helps dispel gas and regulates the functioning of the gall bladder. It also lessens intestinal contractions, nausea and vomiting. It can relieve headaches and stomach aches, and can alleviate inflammation. It also contains anti-cancer substances and can help inhibit depression. Calcium, which is most important in the development of healthy bones and teeth, is abundant in ginger.

Both young and ripe gingers are used in cooking. The latter is used to neutralize the strong odour of meat and to add aroma to the dishes. Young ginger can be finely sliced and added to various food dishes to enhance the taste and aromatic quality. They are sometimes beautifully carved and pickled to be eaten as a condiment.

Ka-min *(Turmeric)*

It helps to dispel gas and prevent ulcers. It regulates the digestive system and lessens intestinal contraction and can be used to treat colic and distension of the abdomen.

Turmeric is added as an ingredient in yellow curry and can be used either fresh or in powdered form.

Prik-chi-fah *(Spur Chilli)*

In addition to boosting the appetite, spur chilli also acts as a tonic for the system. It dispels gas, phlegm, urine and can also be used to treat indigestion. Vitamin A, an essential element for good sight, can also be found in spur chilli.

Fresh spur chillies are sliced and added to curries and stir-fried dishes to give colour and spiceness. Dried spur chillies are also another essential ingredient in making curry pastes.

Prik-khi-noo *(Bird Chilli)*

Bird Chilli helps with digestion and promotes good appetite. It also dispels gas, induces sweat and can cleanse pores to give clear complexion. Bird chilli contains anti-cancer substances as well as fibre, calcium, phosphorus, iron, vitamins A, B1, B2 and C.

Fresh Bird Chilli comes in both red and green and are typically used in dips and curries for pungency. Dried chillies are roasted and ground into powder and used for adding to any types of food to enhance the flavour and increase the spiciness.

Bai-kra-wan *(Bay Leaf)*

It is used to dispel gas and phlegm and to treat rheumatism. It also helps to regulate the stomach.

Bay leaves are used in meat dishes such as mussaman curry and can be added as a garnish to enhance the aroma.

Look-kra-wan *(Cardamon)*

It is used as a tonic to dispel gas in the stomach and to discharge phlegm. It is also used to treat diarrhea, distension of the abdomen, colic and indigestion.

Cardamon seeds are used in mussaman and yellow curry pastes. Whole cardamon can be added to curries to enhance the aroma.

Kan-plu *(Clove)*

Clove is used as a remedy for indigestion because it dispels gas and aids digestion. Cloves are roasted to release their aroma and used as an ingredient in curry pastes.

Dok-jan-tade *(Mace)*

Mace promotes appetite and dispels gas. It is also used as a tonic for digestion and for the heart.

It is used to neautralize the strong odour in meat dishes such as beef curries or various beef soups.

Look-jan-tade *(Nutmeg)*

It is used to treat distension of the abdomen and to help with digestion. It is a nourishing tonic and prevents diarrhea and certain diseases of the stomach and the intestine. Nutmeg is usually roasted and ground into powered form and used for meat dishes, for the same pupose as mace.

Pouy-guk *(Star Anise)*

Star anise helps dispel gas and phlegm. Additionally, it can also serve as a laxative and is thus effective for treating constipation and distention of the abdomen. It is used in *Palo* or spicy Thai casseroles or in steamed dishes to give extra aroma to the food. Roasting increases its aroma and is often used together with cinnamon.

Ob-chey *(Cinnamon)*

It induces sweat to give freshness and acts as a remedy for exhaustion. It also dispels gas and distension of the abdomen. It is used to neutralize odour in meat dishes such as *Palo* and mussamun curry paste.

Prik - thai - dum *(Black Peppercorn)*

It promotes appetite, dispels wind and reduces fever. Used in various meat dishes to neutralize the strong odour, black peppercorn enhances the aroma of the food to make it more appetizing. This is especially true with black Peppercorn, which is more aromatic than the white peppercorn. They should be roasted until expanded to fully draw out the aroma.

Prik-thai-kao *(White Peppercorn)*

It helps dispels gas and helps relieve distension of the abdomen. It also acts as a tonic to promote appetite as well as to dispel sweat and urine. It is used in meat dishes not only to increase the aroma and flavour but also as a food preservative.

Look-pak-chee *(Coriander Seed)*

It dispels gas and relieves colic from intestinal contraction. It also gives freshness to the breath. Coriander seeds are typically used in meat dishes to neutralize the strong odour and give special aroma to those dishes. Coriander seeds are used in many curry pastes.

Yi-rah *(Cumin, Fennel)*

It dispels gas, relieves stomachache and distension of the abdomen. It can also aid indigestion. Cumin seeds should be first roasted to bring out their aromas. They are usually used in meat dishes for neutralizing strong odour and also form an important ingredient in making curry pastes.

Apart from the herbs decribed above, garlic, coriander roots, and peppercorn can be ground togther to form a blended paste locally known as **Sam Gleu**, literally translating to **the three pals**. Such paste is used to add aroma and taste in many types of Thai dishes. Sometimes the paste is used for stir-fried dishes or for marinating raw meat prior to frying to enhance its aromatic flavour.

Curry Pastes Used in Thai Cooking

One of the most essential ingredients used in Thai cooking is curry paste. Key in making curries and stir-fried dishes, preparation of food with curry pastes are categorized as follows:

Nam - prik Kaeng Som (Hot and Sour Curry Paste)

Nam - prik Kaeng Phed (Red Curry Paste-Phed)

Nam - prik Kaeng Pa (Spicy Red Curry Paste)

Nam - prik Kaeng Keow - wan (Green Curry Paste)

Nam - prik Kaeng Mus-sa-man (Mussaman Curry Paste)

Nam - prik Kaeng Pa-nang (Panang Curry Paste)

Nam - prik - pow (Roasted Chilli Paste)

Sam-gleu (The Three Pals)

30   30   31

31   32   32

33   33

Nam-prik Kaeng Som

(Hot and Sour Curry Paste)

Ingredients

6 dried red chillies

3 tablespoons shallots, sliced

1 teaspoon garlic, sliced

1 teaspoon shrimp paste

50 g. fish or prawns, boiled

1 teaspoon salt

Preparation

1   Remove seeds from the dried chillies, cut to pieces and then soak in water until soft. Squeeze dry.
2   Pound the dried chillies with salt to a fine paste. Add shallots and garlic, and continue to pound to a smooth paste.
3   Add shrimp paste, boiled fish or prawns and pound until well blended together. Set aside ready for making the curry.

Nam-prik Kaeng Phed

(Red Curry Paste-Phed)

Ingredients

5 dried red chillies

1 teaspoon chopped galangal

1 tablespoon lemongrass, finely sliced

½ teaspoon kaffir lime zests, finely sliced

1 tablespoon coriander roots, finely chopped

2 tablespoons shallots, coarsely sliced

3 tablespoons garlic, coarsely sliced

1 teaspoon shrimp paste

½ teaspoon peppercorns

1 teaspoon salt

Preparation

1   Remove seeds from the dried chillies, cut to pieces and then soak in water until soft. Squeeze dry.
2   Pound salt, galangal, lemongrass, kaffir lime zests, coriander roots and peppercorns together to make fine paste.
3   Add shallots and garlic. Continue pounding until smooth, then add shrimp paste and mixed together into a smooth paste. Set aside ready for making the curry.

Nam-prik Kaeng Pa

(Spicy Red Curry Paste)

Ingredients

7 dried red chillies

1 teaspoon galangal, finely sliced

1 tablespoon lemongrass, finely sliced

½ teaspoon kaffir lime zests, finely sliced

1 tablespoon coriander roots, finely chopped

3 tablespoons shallots, coarsely sliced

¼ cup garlic, coarsely sliced

1 teaspoon shrimp paste

¼ teaspoon peppercorns

1 teaspoon salt

Preparation

1   Remove seeds from the dried chillies, cut to pieces and then soak in water until soft. Squeeze dry.

2   Pound the chillies and salt together to a fine paste, add galangal, lemongrass, kaffir lime zests, coriander roots and peppercorns. Continue to pound until all ingredients are mixed together.

3   Add shallots and garlic and continue to pound together. Then add the shrimp paste and pound to a smooth paste. Set aside ready for use in making the curry.

Nam-prik Kaeng Keow - wan

(Green Curry Paste)

Ingredients

2 green spur chillies

3 yellow spur chillies

10 bird chillies

1 teaspoon galangal, finely sliced

1 tablespoon lemongrass, finely sliced

½ teaspoon kaffir lime zests, finely sliced

3 tablespoons coriander roots, finely chopped

2 tablespoons shallots, coarsely sliced

¼ cup garlic, coarsely sliced

1 teaspoon shrimp paste

1 teaspoon roasted and powdered coriander seeds

½ teaspoon roasted and powdered cumin seeds

1 teaspoon salt

Preparation

1   Pound all the three kinds of chillies with salt into a fine paste, then add galangal, lemongrass, kaffir lime zests and coriander roots. Continue pounding until well mixed.

2   Add shallots and garlic, followed by shrimp paste, coriander seeds, cumin seeds and pound until all ingredients are well mixed into a smooth paste. Set aside for use in making the curry.

Nam-prik Kaeng Mus-sa-man
(Mussaman Curry Paste)

Ingredients

4 dried red chillies

½ teaspoon galangal, finely sliced and roasted

1 tablespoon lemongrass, finely sliced and roasted

3 tablespoons shallots, roasted and coarsely sliced

¼ cup garlic, roasted and coarsely sliced

1 teaspoon shrimp paste, roasted

2 tablespoons coriander seeds, roasted and powdered

1 teaspoon cumin seeds, roasted and powdered

2 cloves, roasted

¼ teaspoon peppercorns

1 teaspoon salt

Preparation

1   Remove seeds from the dried chillies, cut to pieces and then soak in water until soft. Squeeze dry.
2   Pound the dried chillies and salt together into a fine paste, then add galangal, lemongrass and peppercorns. Continue to pound.
3 Add shallots and garlic. Continue pounding, then add coriander seeds, cumin seeds, cloves and shrimp paste. Pound into a smooth paste. Set aside ready for use in making the curry.

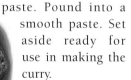

Nam-prik Kaeng Pa-nang
(Panang Curry Paste)

Ingredients

7 dried red chillies

1 teaspoon chopped galangal

1 tablespoon lemongrass, finely sliced

½ teaspoon kaffir lime zests, finely sliced

1 tablespoon coriander roots, finely chopped

3 tablespoons shallots, coarsely sliced

¼ cup garlic, coarsely sliced

2 teaspoons coriander seeds, roasted and powdered

1 teaspoon cumin seeds, roasted and powdered

2 tablespoons peanuts, roasted and pounded

1 teaspoon shrimp paste

¼ teaspoon peppercorns

1 teaspoon salt

Preparation

1   Remove seeds from the dried chillies, cut to pieces and then soak in water until soft. Squeeze dry.
2   Pound chillies with salt into fine paste, add galangal and lemongrass, kaffir lime zests, coriander roots and peppercorns. Continue pounding.
3   Add shallots and garlic and pound into fine paste. Finally add shrimp paste, powdered coriander seeds, cumin seeds and peanuts. Continue to pound all ingredients into a smooth paste. Set aside ready for making the curry.

Nam-prik-pow

(Roasted Chilli Paste)

Ingredients

1 cup dried shrimps, ground
2 cups garlic, sliced and deep fried until golden brown
2 cups shallots, sliced and deep fried until golden brown
1 cup dried red chillies, deep fried
¼ cup tamarind concentrate
¼ cup palm sugar
¼ cup fish sauce
¼ cup vegetable oil

Preparation

1. Pound the fried garlic and shallots slices together with the dried red chillies into a smooth paste.
2. Pour vegetable oil into a pan and stir-fry the chilli paste from 1 until fragrant. Season with palm sugar, fish sauce and tamarind concentrate.

Sam-gleu

(The Three Pals)

Ingredients

3 coriander roots, chopped
5 cloves garlic, chopped
1 teaspoon peppercorns

Preparation

Pound all the ingredients together into a fine paste.
Set aside for use as a marinade for meat or add to food for aromatic smell and delicious taste.

Tip

Peppercorns can be substituted by 1 teaspoon of powdered pepper.

It can be seen that various curry pastes used in Thai cooking have similar ingredients. The quantities used, however, vary to give distinctiveness to each curry paste. Some spices are added to give different colour, aroma and flavour. All recipes for different kinds of curries are therefore, assembled here for references.

36

38

40

42

44

46

48

50

52

54

56

58

60

62

64

Single – course Dish

Traditionally, it was common for an extended Thai family to gather for meals at a large, often round, table. A typical meal would comprise three to five main dishes, depending on the size of the family. However, modern and changing lifestyles have altered this tradition. As more women now hold full-time jobs, less time is spent on cooking. Eating preferences and patterns have therefore adapted to suit modern trends. Many Thais now prefer a plate of rice topped with a single choice of curry or other toppings. These single-dishes are less time consuming and more convenient to prepare. Increasingly popular among diners, opting for a quick and convenient meal over a full course cuisine, these single course dishes are, nowadays, commonly found on the menu of most Thai restaurants. Typical examples include fried noodles with gravy *(Kuay Teow Rad Na)*, Thai stir-fried noodles *(Kuay Teow Phad Thai)* or stir-fried noodles with black soy sauce *(Kuay Teow Pad Si Ew)*. Rice dishes include fried rice *(Khao Phad)*, steamed chicken rice *(Khao Mun Kai)*, rice with barbecued pork *(Khao Moo Daeng)* and spicy fried rice with basil *(Khao Phad Kaprow)*.

Sen - Jan Phad Poo

(Fried Chandhaburi Rice Noodles with Crabmeat)

Ingredients

200 g. dry Chandhaburi rice noodles
2 medium sized crabs, cut into pieces
$\frac{1}{3}$ cup palm sugar
$\frac{1}{3}$ cup tamarind concentrate
$\frac{1}{3}$ cup fish sauce
$\frac{1}{2}$ cup water
2 cups bean sprouts
$\frac{1}{2}$ cup chinese chives, cut into 1 inch pieces
chilli paste for frying
vegetable oil for deep - frying crabs
cucumbers, sliced length - wise
or other fresh greens as a side dish

Preparation

1 Soak the noodles in water for about 10 - 15 minutes. Drain and set aside.
2 Deep fry crabs until golden brown. Drain and set aside.
3 Fry the chilli paste in four table-spoons of oil until fragrant. Season with fish sauce, palm sugar and tamarind concentrate. Simmer, add water and simmer until thickened.
4 Add crabmeat to the chilli sauce, set aside. Fry the noodles until soft, then return the crabmeat to the pan and mix well. Served with cucumbers or other green vegetables.

Ingredients
for the Chilli Paste

7 dried red chillies, seeded and soaked until soft
3 dried small hot red chillies, soaked
2 tablespoons garlic, sliced
$\frac{1}{2}$ cup shallots, sliced
1 teaspoon salt

Preparation

Pound chillies with salt into a fine paste. Add garlic and shallots and continue pounding until the mixture is a smooth paste.

Tip
The crab can be substituted by other meat such as lobster, fish or white bean curd.

Serves : 4 persons

Steps

1 Pound all ingredients for chilli paste together until become a smooth paste. Set aside.
2 Deep fry crabmeat until golden brown
3 Stir-fry chilli paste until fragrant, then add the fried crabmeat. Mix well and set aside.
4 Fry Chandhaburi noodles until soft.
   Add the chilli-crab mixture.

Mee – ka – ti

(Rice Vermicelli with Coconut Sauce)

Ingredients

175 g. dry unbleached rice vermicelli
5 cups coconut milk
2 tablespoons salted soya bean paste
$3/4$ cup yellow bean curd, diced
$1/2$ cup minced pork
$1/2$ cup minced prawns
$1/2$ cup shallots, finely chopped
3 $1/2$ tablespoons tamarind concentrate
3 tablespoons granulated sugar
6 tablespoons fish sauce
4 tablespoons tomato ketchup
1 teaspoon dried red chilli powder
coriander leaves and red and yellow chillies, sliced into thin
strips for garnish bean sprouts and chives as a side dish

Preparation Sauce

1   Bring a cup of coconut milk to boil, and set aside.
2   Mix the minced pork and minced prawns in 2 cups of coconut milk and stir well. Then pour this mixture into the boiled coconut milk, stirring until well blended. Return to heat and add shallots, diced bean curd, salted soya beans paste and dried red chilli powder. Season with fish sauce, sugar and tamarind concentrate and set aside to be poured over the vermicelli.

Frying the Vermicelli

1   Pass hot water over the vermicelli. Drain the softened vermicelli and set aside.
2   Bring the remaining 2 cups of coconut milk to boil, and, when the oil surfaces, stir in tomato ketchup until well blended. Add coconut mixture to the softened vermicelli, add bean sprouts and chives. Continue frying until cooked.
3   Serve the vermicelli topped with the prepared sauce and sprinkled with the coriander leaves and shredded red and yellow spur chilli.

Serves : 4 persons

Steps

1   Bring a cup of coconut milk to boil, and when the oil surfaces, set aside.
2   Heat 2 cups of coconut milk with minced pork and minced prawns. Pour the boiled coconut milk into the mixture.
3   Add bean curd, salted soya beans paste and dried red chilli powder. Season and set aside.
4   Bring to boil the remaining coconut milk (2 cups) with tomato ketchup. Then add the vermicelli and mix well.

Kuay - teow Phad Si - ew

(Stir-Fried Noodles with Soy Sauce)

Ingredients

300 g. wide fresh noodles

200 g. pork, sliced

½ cup collard green leaves, cut into pieces

¼ cup carrot, cut into 1 inch pieces

¼ cup baby corns, sliced diagonally

1 tablespoon chopped garlic

2 eggs

3½ tablespoons soy sauce

2½ tablespoons granulated sugar

3 tablespoons vegetable oil

Preparation

1 Mix the soy sauce well into the fresh noodles and set aside.
2 Stir-fry the garlic in oil until golden, add the pork and continue frying until cooked. Add the noodles and kale leaves with all the seasonings. Turning until well mixed.
3 Push the noodles to the side of the wok and add beaten eggs. Once they begin to set, quickly scramble them and stir through the noodles and serve.

Serves : 2 persons

Steps

1 Mix the soy sauce into the fresh noodles.
2 Fry pork and garlic until cooked.
3 Stir-fry the noodles and vegetables with all seasonings.
4 Add eggs and turn quickly until cooked.

Kuay-teow Rad-na Ta-lay

(Stir-Fried Noodles with Seafood in Gravy)

Ingredients

200 g. wide fresh noodles

50 g. fish, cut into bite-size

50 g. squids, cut into bite-size

5 prawns, peeled and deveined

50 g. crabmeat

100 g. collard green leaves, cut into pieces

100 g. baby corns, cut into pieces

100 g. carrots, cut into 2 inches long pieces

1 tablespoon chopped garlic

2 teaspoons Chinese wine

3 cups stock, chicken

1 tablespoon oyster sauce

2 teaspoons soy sauce

1 teaspoon salt

1 teaspoon granulated sugar

4 tablespoons corn starch

1/4 cup water

2 tablespoons vegetable oil for stir-frying

ground pepper to sprinkle

vegetable oil for deep-frying the fresh noodles

Preparation

1 Separate the fresh noodles and fry in a little vegetable oil (medium heat) until golden. Set aside.

2 Mix corn starch with water into a thin paste, set aside.

3 Heat oil in a wok and stir-fry the seafood, followed by kale leaves, baby corns and carrots. Add Chinese wine and stir to mix.

4 Add stock and season with oyster sauce, sugar, salt and soy sauce. Bring to the boil, then stir in the corn starch paste to thicken the gravy. Pour the sauce over the noodles, sprinkle pepper over it and serve.

Serves : 2 persons

Steps

1 Fry the fresh noodles until brown.

2 Add the seafood and fry until cooked.

3 Add all vegetables. Mix all the ingredients together.

4 Pour in the stock and when boiled, stir in the corn starch paste and continue to boil until the sauce thicken.

Kuay – teowPhad ThaiKoongSod

(Thai Stir-Fried Noodles with Prawn)

Ingredients

100 g. (dried weight) Chandhaburi noodles or small rice noodles

6 medium sized prawns, peeled and deveined

½ cup bean curd, diced

4 tablespoons pickled white radish, finely chopped

3 tablespoons vegetable oil

4 tablespoons roasted peanuts, coarsely ground

4 tablespoons palm sugar syrup

4 tablespoons tamarind concentrate

4 tablespoons fish sauce

½ teaspoon dried red chilli powder

2 eggs

1 cup raw bean sprouts

¼ cup chinese chives, cut into 1 inch pieces

fresh vegetables as side dish

Preparation

1 Soak the noodles until soft. Drain.
2 In a wok, fry the bean curd in little oil until golden brown, then add the pickled white radish. Season with palm sugar syrup, fish sauce, tamarind concentrate and dried red chilli powder. Add prawns and continue to fry until they are cooked.
3 Gently fry the softened noodles, add a little water, then push to the side of the wok. Add beaten eggs, and, when they begin to set, quickly scramble them and continue to fry them with bean sprouts and chives. Sprinkle chopped peanuts on top and serve on a plate with fresh vegetables as a side dish.

Tip

The syrup is made from boiling 200 g. of palm sugar and 1 cup of water to the syrupy thickness.

Steps

1 Fry bean curd with pickled white radish and add seasonings. Taste for the desired flavour.
2 Fry remaining ingredients with the noodles.
3 Add eggs and continue frying.
4 Mix in all the vegetables.

Serves : 2 persons

Kuay - teow - lod

(Stuffed Noodles)

Ingredients

400 g. fresh sheet rice noodles, cut into 3 x 3 inch square

1 ½ cups fresh bamboo shoot, diced and blanched

½ cup carrots, diced

½ cup bean curd, diced

½ cup dried shrimp

½ cup dried Chinese mushrooms, soaked in water and diced

1 tablespoon garlic, finely chopped

1 tablespoon coriander roots, finely chopped

½ tablespoon ground pepper

¼ cup spring onions and coriander, finely sliced

3 tablespoons fish sauce

2 tablespoons soy sauce

2 tablespoons brown sugar

3 tablespoons vegetable oil

chilli sauce

Preparation

1 Grind garlic, coriander roots and peppercorns to a fine paste. Fry in hot oil until aromatic.

2 Add the mushrooms, dried shrimps, bean curd, bamboo shoot and carrots. Season and continue to fry until well mixed. Set aside.

3 Spread the noodle sheet on a plate and spoon the fried mixture on to the middle of the sheet and fold over. Serve with chilli sauce.

Serves: 4 persons

Steps

1 Stir-fry coriander, garlic and pepper paste with bean curd.

2 Add the dried shrimps, mushrooms and the rest of the ingredients, continue to fry.

3 Spoon the mixture on the middle of the noodle sheet.

4 Fold the noodle over the stuffing.

Kuay - teow Moo - sub

(Stir-Fried Noodles with Ground Pork)

Ingredients

250g. wide fresh noodles

150 g. minced pork

$\frac{1}{2}$ cup onion, sliced thinly

1 - 2 tomatoes, diced

$\frac{1}{4}$ cups carrots, diced

$\frac{1}{4}$ cup baby corns, cut into pieces

3 tablespoons cooked peas

3 tablespoons cooked diced pumpkin

$1\frac{1}{2}$ cups stock, vegetable

2 tablespoons dried preserved chopped cabbage

$\frac{1}{2}$ tablespoon curry powder

3 tablespoons vegetable oil

1 tablespoon chopped garlic

2 tablespoons soy sauce

1 - 2 teaspoons black soy sauce

$1\frac{1}{2}$ tablespoons granulated sugar

$\frac{1}{4}$ teaspoon salt

4 tablespoons corn starch

$\frac{1}{4}$ cup water to mix with the corn starch

1 - 2 lettuces

Tip

Ground pork can be substituted by other meat such as beef or chicken of the same amount.

Serves : 2 persons

Steps

1 Stir-fry the noodles in a wok.
2 Stir-fry onion with minced pork.
3 Add all the vegetables, continue frying.
4 Add the stock and corn starch paste.

Preparation

1 Mix black soy sauce with the noodle and stir-fry with a little oil. Leave to cool, then arrange on plate over the lettuce leaves.
2 Fry the garlic until golden, add onion and minced pork. Followed by the dried preserved chopped cabbage, tomatoes, carrots, baby corns, peas, pumpkin and curry powder. Pour in the stock and bring to boil. Season with soy sauce and sugar. Taste for flavour. Then stir in the corn starch paste and continue to cook until thickened before pouring the mixture over the noodles.

Ka - nom - jeenNam - ya Hed

(Chinese Rice-Flour Vermicelli with Spicy Mushroom Sauce)

Ingredients for the Curry Paste

7 - 8 dried red chillies

5 - 6 shallots, cut

2 tablespoons cut garlic

1 teaspoon galangal, sliced

1 cup fingerroots, skinned and sliced finely

2 tablespoons lemongrass, finely sliced

Preparation

Pound all ingredients into a fine paste, set aside.

Ingredient s for the Spicy Mushroom Sauce

6 cups coconut milk

500 g. angel mushrooms, finely chopped

6 tablespoons fish sauce

2 cups curry paste

Chinese rice-flour vermicelli

vegetables such as bean sprouts, string beans, sweet basil leaves and shredded cabbage

Steps

1 Pound the curry paste smooth.
2 Mix together with coconut milk.
3 Add angel mushrooms and boil until cooked.
4 Season with fish sauce and sugar.

Preparation

Mix the curry paste with coconut milk and bring to a boil. Then add the angel mushrooms and season with fish sauce and sugar. When boiled, spoon on to the Chinese rice-flour vermicelli and serve with vegetables of your choice.

Tip

Canned tuna or other fish with soft and fluffy flesh can be used instead of mushrooms. The taste of the sauce will improve greatly.

Serves : 4 persons

Kuay - teow Kua Kai

(Stir-Fried Noodles with Chicken)

Ingredients

300 g. wide fresh noodles

200 g. chicken, cut to bite-size

2 eggs

3 tablespoons vegetable oil

2 tablespoons dried preserved chopped cabbage

2 - 3 tablespoons oyster sauce

2 tablespoons all-purpose sauce

2 tablespoons granulated sugar

ground pepper, shredded spring onions and lettuce

chilli sauce

Preparation

1   In a wok stir-fry chicken with dried preserved chopped cabbage until well cooked. Then add the noodles and turn over quickly (use medium heat.)

2   Season with all-purpose sauce, oyster sauce and sugar. Push the noodles to the side of the wok, add beaten eggs and quickly scramble. Stir-fry the eggs, chicken and noodles together until aromatic. Dish out on a plate over lettuce leaves and sprinkle with a pepper and sliced spring onions. Serve with chilli sauce.

Serves : 2 persons

Steps

1   Stir-fry dried pickled chopped cabbage until aromatic.

2   Add chicken and continue frying.

3   Add noodles, turning until well mixed.

4   Add the eggs and fry until cooked.

Kuay – teow Phad Kee Mow

(Stir-Fried Spicy Noodles)

Ingredients

300 g. wide fresh noodles

8 - 10 medium sized prawns, peeled and deveined

1/4 cup carrots, cut and blanched

1/4 cup baby corns, sliced diagonally and blanched

10 bird chillies, coarsely chopped

1 - 2 tablespoons garlic, finely chopped

3 tablespoons vegetable oil

1 1/2 cups holy basil or sweet basil leaves

1/4 cup green peppercorns

3 - 4 tablespoons fish sauce

1 tablespoon granulated sugar

2 each of red and yellow spur chillies, sliced

Preparation

1 Put the oil in a wok and stir-fry the chillies and garlic until golden. Then add the prawns and continue frying until they are cooked. The carrots and baby corns are then added, followed by the noodles, turning them quickly. Season with fish sauce and sugar.

2 Add green peppercorns, basil leaves and sliced chillies. When all the ingredients are well mixed dish and serve.

Tip

The amount of chillies used can be reduced as desired.

Serves : 2 persons

Steps

1 Stir-fry chillies and garlic until golden.

2 Add the prawns and continue frying until cooked.

3 Add the noodles and seasonings.

4 Add the vegetables.

Khao-phad Nam-prik-pow Ta-lay

(Fried Rice with Roasted Chilli Paste and Seafood)

Ingredients

3 cups cooked unpolished rice

6 - 8 medium sized prawns, peeled

200 g. squids, cut into pieces

$\frac{1}{4}$ cup carrots, diced

$\frac{1}{4}$ cup baby corns, cut diagonally

$\frac{1}{4}$ cup asparagus spears, cut into pieces

$\frac{1}{4}$ cup green beans, cut into pieces

$\frac{1}{2}$ cup cauliflower, cut into pieces

3 tablespoons roasted chilli paste (page 33)

2 tablespoons chopped garlic

3 tablespoons vegetable oil

2 teaspoons granulated sugar

$\frac{1}{4}$ teaspoon salt

1 - 2 tablespoons fish sauce

Preparation

1 Mix the cooked rice together with the roasted chilli paste. Set aside.

2 Put the oil in a wok and stir-fry the garlic until golden. Add the seafood and vegetables. Continue frying until cooked, season with sugar, fish sauce and salt and serve.

Tip

Other meat or vegetables can be used instead as desired.

Serves : 2 persons

Steps

1 Mix the cooked rice with roasted chilli paste until well blended.

2 Stir-fry the squids and prawns until cooked.

3 Add the vegetables.

4 Add the chilli-rice, until well mixed.

Khao - phad Poo

(Fried Rice with Crabmeat)

Ingredients

4 cups cooked unpolished rice
$\frac{3}{4}$ cup crabmeat, cooked and shelled
2 eggs
$\frac{1}{3}$ cup onion, diced
3 tablespoons soy sauce
$\frac{1}{2}$ tablespoon all purpose sauce
2 tablespoons granutated sugar
3 tablespoons vegetable oil
2 tablespoons chopped garlic
ground pepper
sliced spring onions and cucumbers

Preparation

1 Put a little vegetable oil in a wok and stir-fry garlic until golden. Add onion followed by crabmeat. Push to the size of the wok.
2 With the remaining oil, scramble the eggs until cooked, then add the cooked rice. Season with soy sauce, all purpose sauce and sugar. Continue to stir-fry until well mixed. Dish out on a plate and sprinkle with ground pepper and sliced spring onions. Serve with cucumbers.

Steps

1 Stir-fry garlic and onion until golden.
2 Add the crabmeat, continue frying.
3 Add the beaten eggs and scramble until cooked.
4 Put in the cooked rice and stir until well mixed.

Tip

The crab meat can be substituted by chicken or pork to get more variety of fried rice-namely *Khao Phad Kai* or *Khao Phad Moo* or Fried Rice with Chicken or Pork.

Serves : 2 - 3 persons

Steps

1 Finely chop the pork.
2 Stir-fry the pork until cooked.
3 Add the remaining ingredients and cooked rice, stir-fry until well mixed.
4 Put the fried rice in an earthen casserole pot and cook slowly.

Khao – ob Phuek

(Baked Taro Rice)

Ingredients

3 cups cooked unpolished rice
½ cup minced pork
1 cup boiled taro, diced
4 dried Chinese mushrooms, soaked in water and cut into pieces
¼ cup cashew nuts
4 tablespoons dried shrimps
½ teaspoon salt
2 teaspoons soy sauce
2 teaspoons granulated sugar
2 teaspoons butter
3 tablespoons vegetable oil
½ teaspoon ground pepper

Preparation

Pour vegetable oil into a wok, stir-fry the minced pork, followed by the remaining ingredients. Stir until well mixed. Then, put in an earthen casserole pot cook over low heat until the rice is aromatic and cooked, ready to serve.

Tip

The rice can be cooked in a pan covered with a lid instead of the earthen casserole pot.

Serves : 2 persons

Khao - phad Sa - moon - prai

(Fried Rice with Herbs)

Ingredients

2½ cups cooked unpolished rice

½ cup salted tiny fishs, crisply fried

1 tablespoon garlic, finely chopped

2 tablespoons galangal, finely chopped

2 tablespoons lemongrass, finely sliced

2 tablespoons kaffir lime leaves, finely sliced

3 tablespoons cooked mung beans

1½ tablespoons white sesame seeds, roasted

2 tablespoons soy sauce

1 teaspoon granulated sugar

1 tablespoon vegetable oil

fresh vagetables

Preparation

1   In a wok, stir-fry garlic, galangal, lemongrass and kaffir lime leaves with vegetable oil until golden (low heat).

2   Add cooked rice, crispy small salted fishs and cooked mung beans. Continue frying.

3   Season with soy sauce and sugar. Sprinkle with roasted sesame seeds, dish out and serve with vegetables.

Tip

The amount of herbs such as galangal, lemongrass and kaffir lime leaves used can be increased as desired.

Serves : 2 persons

Steps

1   Stir-fry garlic, galangal, lemongrass and kaffir lime leaves until golden.

2   Add cooked rice.

3   Put in crispy small salted fishs and cooked mung beans. Continue frying until well mixed.

4   Sprinkle roasted sesame seeds on top.

Khao - phad Sup - pa - rod

(Fried Rice with Pineapple)

Ingredients

4 cups cooked jasmine rice
10 prawns, peeled and deveined
100 g. boiled pork, diced
100 g. squids, cut diagonally
1½ cups pineapple, diced
¼ cup onion, diced
¼ cup tomato, diced
2 tablespoons garlic, finely chopped
1 tablespoon soy sauce
2 teaspoons granulated sugar
2 - 3 tablespoons vegetable oil
ground pepper and sliced spring onions for garnish

Preparation

1 Stir-fry the garlic in vegetable oil until golden. Add the prawns, pork and squids fry until cooked. Then add the onion, tomato and pineapple.
2 Fry the cooked rice. Season with sugar and soy sauce. Sprinkle with ground pepper and sliced spring onions.

Serves : 4 persons

Steps

1 Stir-fry the garlic until golden.
2 Add the prawns, pork and squids.
3 Add vegetables.
4 Put in the jasmine rice and fry until well mixed

Stir – Fry (Phad)

This is the process of cooking with a small amount of oil. Stir-fried dishes can be bland or spicy, with clear soy sauce, oyster sauce, all-purpose seasoning, and sugar as ingredients for bland dishes. These dishes usually have a salty taste with a hint of sweetness from the meat and vegetables used. More sugar can be added to enhance the flavour further. As with the hot and spicy stir fried dishes, curry pastes are typically

68

70

72

74

76

78

80

82

84

86

88

90

92

94

96

98

used, which gives an even more salty and spicier taste. Some sweetness may also be derived from some of the ingredients used.

A common method for stir-frying is to cook the meat separately first and then adding vegetables for a quick fry. High heat is recommended for frying as certain kinds of vegetables can become tough and discoloured with the length of cooking time. Slow cooking vegetables such as carrots, baby corns, and asparagus should be scalded in hot water first and then immediately soaked in cold water to retain good colouring when stir-frying. As for the hot and spicy stir-fries, the proper method is to fry the curry paste with oil first until fragrant before adding meat and vegetables.

Deep - Fry (Tod)

At the start of the cooking process the oil must be extremely hot to prevent the food becoming greasy but then, the heat should be lowered slightly so that the food is thoroughly cooked without being burnt on the outside.

Drier foods tends to be less greasy when deep-fried. For example, bread used for making toasts with toppings would be less greasy if they were previously baked or air-dried. The size of the food stuff being fried is also a factor. Thicker slices take longer to cook than thinner pieces. In order to save cooking time and lessen greasiness in the food, it is recommended to pre-cook the food first by steaming prior to frying.

Steaming (Nung)

This is the process of cooking with steam. A double boiler is used for this method of cooking, with the lower pot containing boiling water and the upper pot containing the food itself. The heat required is approximately 100°C. Nowadays, pressure cookers are available which shorten the cooking time considerably. Meat becomes tender much quicker than the conventional method of boiling or steaming.

Grill, Broil (Yang)

With this method, food is cooked over flame. A grill can be used to flip the food and broil both sides.

Roast (Ob)

With this method, meat is placed into a pot with closed lid and cooked over low heat until tender or fully cooked. Alternatively, some types of food may be roasted in a conventional oven.

Koong - ob Woon -sen Prik - thai - dum

(Baked Glass Vermicelli Casserole with Black Peppercorn Prawn)

Ingredients

4 medium giant fresh water prawns

2 cups unbleached glass vermicelli, soaked in water

2 dried Chinese mushrooms, soaked in water and sliced

2 teaspoons black peppercorns, crushed

3 slices ginger

2 coriander roots, crushed

3 cloves garlic, crushed

1/4 cup celery, cut into pieces

2 tablespoons soy sauce

1 teaspoon all purpose sauce

1 tablespoon oyster sauce

2 teaspoons granulated sugar

2 teaspoons vegetable oil

1/4 cup stock, chicken

Preparation

1 Mix together the vermicelli with black pepper-corns, soy sauce, all purpose sauce, oyster sauce, sugar and vegetable oil. Set aside.
2 Place the slices of ginger, garlic, coriander roots at the bottom of an earthen casserole pot. Then put in the prawns followed by the mushrooms and topped with the vermicelli. Add the stock, close the lid, cook over low heat for about 10 minutes.
3 Open lid and stir lightly, then add celery and cook 3 minutes. Serve immediately.

Steps

1 Put ginger, garlic and coriander roots in an earthen casserole pot.
2 Add the prawns.
3 Mix all the seasonings into the vermicelli.
4 Put the seasoned vermicelli into the pot and place over low heat until cooked.

Tip

This dish will be more aromatic and delicious if the pot is lined with thin sliced of lard.

Serves : 2 persons

Ho – mok Ta – lay

(Steamed Seafood Curry)

Ingredients

400 g. Sea bass, cut into pieces

1½ cups coconut milk

1 tablespoon rice flour

1 egg

3 tablespoons kaffir lime leaves, finely sliced

2 tablespoons coriander leaves

2 red spur chillies, sliced into thin strips

1 tablespoon fish sauce

50 g. red curry paste (page 30)

1 cup morinda leaves (bai yor), white

Chinese cabbage (sliced and blanched)

sweet basil leaves for lining the

receptacle and garnish

Tip

If the fish curry is wrapped in aluminum foil or banana leaves and broiled or roasted, this dish is called "Ngob Talay"

Serves : 4 persons

Preparation

1 Mix curry paste into half of the coconut milk, stirring until well blended. Add the fish, egg and fish sauce and mix together. Then gradually add the rice flour and the remaining coconut milk, stirring gently.

2 Line the bottom of the receptacles with one kind of vegetable. Spoon the fish curry mixture on top of the vegetable and steam over boiling water for about 10 minutes. Remove from heat and add the coconut cream topping, garnish with coriander leaves, shredded kaffir lime leaves and strips of red spur chilli. Continue to steam for another 5 minutes and serve.

Steps

1 Line the bottom of the banana leaves or ceramic receptacle with vegetable.

2 Mix the curry paste and half of the coconut milk together.

3 Add fish, egg, fish sauce and rice flour to the remaining coconut milk.

4 Spoon the fish curry mixture into the vegetable-lined receptacle.

Coconut Cream Topping

¾ cup coconut cream

(the thickest on top of the coconut milk)

1 tablespoon rice flour

Preparation

Mix the rice flour with the coconut cream and stir over the heat until thickened. Set aside for use.

Khai Look - khuey

(Thai Deviled Egg)

Ingredients

3 boiled chicken or duck eggs

¼ cup palm sugar

2 tablespoons fish sauce

2 tablespoons tamarind concentrate

2 tablespoons crisp fried shallots

2 tablespoons dried red chillies, sliced thinly

vegetable oil for deep - frying

coriander leaves and thin strips of red chillies for garnishing

Preparation

1   Fry the eggs in very hot oil (medium heat) until golden brown all over. Drain and arrange on a plate. Deep-Fry the sliced chillies and set aside to cool.

2   Dissolve sugar over the heat with fish sauce and tamarind concentrate. Continue stirring until of syrupy consistency, then pour the sauce over the eggs. Garnish with crisp fried sliced shallots, fried dried red chillies, coriander leaves and red chilli strips.

Serves : 4 persons

Steps

1   Peel the boiled eggs.

2   Fry them in hot oil until golden brown.

3   Halve each egg into 2 pieces.

4   Boil the palm sugar with other seasonings until syrupy.

Pla Rad Prik

(Crispy Fish with Chilli Sauce)

Ingredients

350 g. Sea bass, cut into rectangular pieces

1/4 cup all purpose flour

1 cup crisp-fried holy basil leaves

vegetable oil for deep-frying

dried red spur chillies

Preparation

1 Dip the fish in flour and deep-fry in hot oil (medium heat) until golden and crisp. Drain and set aside.

2 Arrange the fried fish onto a plate and pour the chilli sauce all over. Garnish with strips of chillies. Serve with crisp basil leaves.

Ingredients for the Chilli Sauce

1/2 cup garlic, finely chopped

3 tablespoons vegetable oil

1/2 teaspoon salt

1/2 cup granulated sugar

1/2 cup vinegar

2 tablespoons fish sauce

1/4 cup red and yellow spur chillies, coarsely chopped

Preparation

Stir-fry the chillies and garlic until golden.
Add all other ingredients and stir over heat until thickened. Set aside to be poured over the fried fish.

Steps

1 Cut the fish into rectangular pieces.

2 Dip the fish in flour and deep-fry until golden brown and crisp.

3 Stir-fry the chillies and garlic until golden.

4 Add the seasonings to the chillies and garlic and boil until thickened.

Tip

If the fish is tossed in dry flour before frying, it will not stick to the bottom of the pan.

Serves : 2 persons

Kai Tod Kruenz - ted

(Fried Spiced Chicken)

Ingredients

500 g. chicken upper wings

2 tablespoons chopped garlic

2 teaspoons black peppercorns, crushed

1 tablespoon paprika

1 teaspoon curry powder

4 tablespoons oyster sauce

2 tablespoons soy sauce

1 tablespoon granulated sugar

½ teaspoon salt

3 tablespoons vegetable oil

4 tablespoons all purpose flour

5 - 6 lemongrass, sliced and crisp-fried

kaffir lime leaves, sliced and crisp-fried

vegetable oil for deep-frying

Preparation

1 Wash the chicken wings. Marinate them in all the ingredients and let stand for 30 minutes.
2 Deep-fry the marinated chicken until golden brown (medium heat). Drain and serve with the crisp kaffir lime leaves and lemongrass slices.

Tip

Crispy fried shredded Kale leaves can be used to accompany the chicken instead of crispy kaffir lime leaves.

Serves : 4 persons

Steps

1 Marinate chicken wings in all the ingredients.
2 Add the flour and leave for 30 minutes.
3 Deep-fry the chicken wings until golden brown.
4 Fry the kaffir lime leaves until crisp.

Phad Prik - kaeng Ta - lay

(Stir-Fried Seafood with Curry Paste)

Ingredients

10 - 12 medium sized prawns, peeled and deveined

200 g. squids, cut diagonally

1 cup string beans, cut and blanched

2 tablespoons granulated sugar

3 - 4 tablespoons fish sauce

$\frac{1}{4}$ cup red curry paste (page 30)

3 - 4 tablespoons vegetable oil

2 tablespoons kaffir lime leaves, finely sliced for garnish

1 each of red and yellow spur chillies, sliced diagonally

Preparation

1 Stir-fry the curry paste until aromatic. Season with sugar and fish sauce, continue frying.

2 Add the prawns and squids, fry until cooked, then add the string beans. Garnish with the chillies and kaffir lime leaves.

Serves : 4 persons

Steps

1 Blanch the beans and set aside.

2 Stir-fry the curry paste until aromatic.

3 Add the squids and prawns and continue to fry until cooked.

4 Add the blanched beans, turning until well mixed.

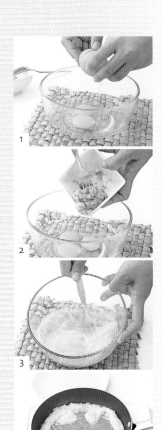

Khai – jiaw Koong Sub

(Mixed Prawn Omelette)

Ingredients

3 eggs

½ cup minced prawns

2 teaspoons fish sauce

½ cup oil for deep-frying

coriander leaves and red spur chillies for garnish

Preparation

Break the eggs into a bowl, add the minced prawns and fish sauce. Beat with a fork and fry in hot oil (medium heat).

Tip

The prawns can be substituted with pork or even different kinds of herbs such as sweet basil leaves, holy basil leaves, kaffir lime leaves or sliced spur chillies. The omelette with herbs not only aromatic and full of flavour, but also nutritious.

Serves : 2 persons

Steps

1   Break the eggs into a bowl.
2   Add minced prawns to the eggs.
3   Beat the eggs and prawns until light and fluffy. Add seasonings.
4   Fry until golden.

Pla Tod Kra - tiam

(Fried Garlic Fish)

Ingredients

1 (about 500 g.) red tilapia fish
1/4 cup small clove garlic
1 tablespoon white peppercorns
1 teaspoon salt
vegetable oil for deep-frying

Preparation

1 Pound garlic, peppercorns and salt into a fine paste. Smear this paste all over the fish and leave for about 20 - 30 minutes.
2 Remove the paste and set aside to be fried later. Deep-fry the fish in hot oil (medium heat) until golden brown. Drain.
3 Stir-fry the garlic paste until crisp and golden. Sprinkle over the fried fish. Serve with green mango sauce.

Ingredients for Green Mango Sauce

1/4 cup sour green mango, shredded
1 tablespoon shallots, sliced thinly
2 tablespoons lime juice
3 tablespoons fish sauce
2 teaspoons granulated sugar
1 - 2 teaspoons fresh bird chillies, sliced finely

Preparation

Mix lime juice, fish sauce, sugar and chillies.
Add the mixture to the shredded mango and shallots.
Mix well and serve with the fried fish.

Steps

1 Mix the mango sauce.
2 Pound together garlic, peppercorns and salt.
3 Smear the garlic paste on the fish.
4 Fry the garlic paste removed from the fish until golden.

Tip

Any other kind of fish can be used according to your preference and convenience.

Serves : 3 - 4 persons

Tao - hoo Song - krueng

(Bean Curd with Prawn and Vegetable Topping)

Ingredients

2 tubes soft white bean curd (tofu)

8 - 10   medium sized prawns, peeled and deveined

$\frac{1}{4}$ cup baby corns, cut diagonally

$\frac{1}{2}$ cup straw mushrooms, sliced

$\frac{1}{4}$ cup carrots, diced

$\frac{1}{4}$ cup snow peas

2 tablespoons garlic, chopped

3 tablespoons vegetable oil

2 tablespoons soy sauce

$\frac{1}{2}$ teaspoon salt

2 teaspoons granulated sugar

$\frac{3}{4}$ cup stock, chicken

$\frac{1}{2}$ teaspoon ground pepper

4 tablespoons corn starch

$\frac{1}{4}$ cup water to mix corn starch

$\frac{1}{2}$ cup all purpose flour for coating

vegetable oil for deep-frying

Tip

When the tofu is are dipped in dry flour, it should not be left standing for a long time because the flour will absorb the water from tofu and will not be crispy when fried.

Serves : 4 persons

Preparation

1   Mix corn starch with water to form a paste and set aside.
2   Cut the tofu across into big chunks. Dry and dip in flour to cover all over and fry in hot oil (medium heat) until brown on all sides. Drain and set aside.
3   Stir-fry the garlic until golden. Add the prawns followed by vegetables. Add a little stock, stir until all ingredients are cooked.
4   Season with soy sauce, salt, sugar and ground pepper. When boiled add the corn flour paste to thicken the sauce. Pour over the tofu.

Steps

1   Cut one soft white bean curd into 4 pieces and dry with paper towel.
2   Deep-fry or fry the flour coated tofu until dry.
3   Stir-fry and season the prawns and vegetables.
4   Add stock and when boiled, add the corn starch paste to thicken the sauce.

Pla Preaw Wan

(Sweet and Sour Fish)

Ingredients

2 cups Plaices, filleted and cut into squares
1 cup all purpose flour
½ cup green, red and yellow capsicums, diced into small pieces
¼ cup snow peas
¼ cup onion, diced into small pieces
¼ cup tomatoes, diced into small pieces
¼ cup cucumbers, diced into small pieces
¼ cup carrots, diced into small pieces
¼ cup baby corns, cut diagonally
1 tablespoon vinegar
1 tablespoon fish sauce
1 tablespoon granulated sugar
¼ cup tomato ketchup
1 tablespoon garlic, chopped
2 tablespoons olive oil
¼ cup stock, chicken
vegetable oil for deep-frying

Steps

1 Cut the fish into squares.
2 Dip the fish in flour and fry until golden brown.
3 Stir-fry all the vegetables with seasonings.
4 Add the fried fish to the sauce, turn quickly to mix.

Preparation

1 Dip the fish in flour and fry until golden brown. Drain.
2 Stir-fry the garlic until golden. Add all vegetables and stock. Mix well.
3 Bring vinegar, fish sauce, sugar and tomato ketchup together to a boil, add the fried fish to the sauce, taste and serve.

Tip

If the fish is marinated in salt and ground pepper about 5 - 10 minutes prior being fried, this dish will be more tasty.

Serves : 4 persons

Pla Tod Rad Sauce Bai – ma – krood

(Fried Fish in Kaffir Lime Leaves Sauce)

Ingredients

2 Pomfrets or Plaices	½ tablespoon salt
(about 300 g. each)	¼ cup stock, chicken
1/4 cup all purpose flour	2 tablespoons corn starch
crisp-fried kaffir lime leaves	¼ cup water to mix the corn starch
vegetable oil for deep-frying	2 tablespoons vegetable oil

Preparation

1 Clean and dry the fish. Make diagonal slashes across the fish on both sides. Coat with dry flour and deep-fry in hot oil (medium heat) until golden.
2 Place the fish on a plate and pour the kaffir lime sauce over it. Serve with crisp kaffir lime leaves.

Ingredients for Kaffir Lime Leaves Sauce

4 tablespoons chopped garlic
3 tablespoons chopped onion
3 tablespoons each of green and yellow spur chillies, chopped
3 tablespoons kaffir lime leaves, finely sliced
3 tablespoons oyster sauce
¼ cup vinegar
3 tablespoons fish sauce
1 cup granulated sugar

Preparation

1 Mix water and corn starch into a paste and set aside. Stir-fry garlic together with the chillies in oil until aromatic. Add all the other ingredients, except the corn starch, and bring to a boil.
2 Stir in corn starch paste until the sauce thickens. Add the shredded kaffir lime leaves and put aside to pour over the fish.

Tip

The method of slashing diagonally across the fish helps it cooked more quickly.

Serves : 3 - 4 persons

Steps

1 Put slashes diagonally across the fish.
2 Deep-fry the fish in hot oil until golden brown.
3 Stir-fry the chillies and garlic until aromatic. Ad seasonings and continue to fry until well mixed.
4 Add the corn starch paste to thicken the sauce.

Hoy – shell Phad Nam – prik – pow

(Stir-Fry Scallop in Roasted Chilli Sauce)

Ingredients

500 g. scallops
2 tablespoons chopped garlic
½ cup roasted chilli paste (page 33)
2 tablespoons granulated sugar
2 tablespoons fish sauce
2 tablespoons vegetable oil
½ cup sweet basil leaves
1 red spur chilli, sliced

Preparation

1   Stir-fry garlic in oil until golden. Add the roasted chilli paste followed by scallops, stirring until cooked.
2   Season with sugar and fish sauce.
3   Add the chilli and sweet basil leaves, turning over thoroughly until well mixed and serve.

Tip

Besides scallops, other shell fish such as clams can be used for this dish.

Serves : 2 persons

Steps

1   Stir-fry garlic in oil until golden.
2   Add roasted chilli paste and mix well.
3   Add scallops, fry until cooked, then put in seasonings.
4   Sprinkle with the chilli and sweet basil leaves.

Phad Ka - prow Pla Tu - na

(Stir-Fry Spicy Tuna Basil)

Ingredients

1 can tuna in water, drained
2 tablespoons garlic, chopped finely
2 tablespoons coarsely ground red spur chillies
1 cup holy basil or red basil leaves
2 tablespoons vegetable oil
2 tablespoons soy sauce
1 tablespoon oyster sauce
1 teaspoon granulated sugar
1 each of green and yellow spur chillies, sliced diagonally

Preparation

1 In a wok, heat vegetable oil and stir-fry garlic and ground chillies until golden. Add tuna and continue frying until well mixed.
2 Season with soy sauce, oyster sauce and sugar. Add sliced chillies and basil leaves and when fragrant dish out ready to accompany steaming hot rice.

Serves : 2 persons

Steps

1 Stir-fry spur chillies and garlic until golden brown.
2 Add tuna and continue frying.
3 Season with soy sauce, oyster sauce and sugar.
4 Add basil leaves and fry until cooked.

Tod – mun Pla

(Spicy Fish Cake)

Ingredients

500 g. giant seaperch, scraped

1½ cups string beans or winged beans, sliced thinly

1 egg

1 tablespoon kaffir lime leaves, sliced finely

½ cup red curry paste (page 30)

1 tablespoon granulated sugar

1½ tablespoons fish sauce

½ teaspoon salt

crisp-fried basil leaves

vegetable oil for deep-frying

Preparation

1 Mix the scrapped flesh of the fish with red curry paste and knead until smooth and firm about 10 minutes.

2 Add the beans and continue kneading until well mixed. Then put in the kaffir lime leaves and egg. Season with sugar, salt and fish sauce.

3 Heat oil in a pan, when hot (medium heat), make the fish mixture into small flat round cakes and deep-fryuntil golden brown. Serve with cucumber relish and crisp-fried basil leaves.

Steps

1 Skin and knead the fish to make a paste, mix with red curry paste.

2 Add the beans and kaffir lime leaves.

3 Blend the egg into the mixture.

4 Deep-fry the flat round cakes until golden brown.

Ingredients for the Relish

2 red spur chillies, coarsely ground

1 cup vinegar

1 cup granulated sugar

½ tablespoon salt

¼ cup coarsely ground peanuts

cucumbers, sliced

Preparation

1 Bring sugar, salt and vinegar to the boil and set aside to cool.

2 Add cucumbers, chillies and peanuts to 1. Serve on the side with the fish cake.

Tip

When kneading the fish, place a bowl of ices beneath to give it the soft and firm texture.

Serves : 3 - 4 persons

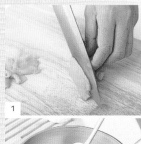

Moo Phad Khing

(Stir-Fry Pork with Ginger)

Ingredients

300 g. fillet of pork, sliced

1¼ cups fresh wood fungus, cut into pieces

½ cup onions, cut into pieces

½ cup young fresh ginger, sliced finely

1 tablespoon chopped garlic

1 tablespoon solted soya beans

2 teaspoons soy sauce

1 - 2 tablespoons granulated sugar

2 tablespoons oyster sauce

3 tablespoons vegetable oil

1 each of green and yellow spur chillies, sliced diagonally

2 spring onions, cut into pieces

Preparation

1 Stir-Fry garlic until golden. Add solted soya beans followed by pork, wood fungus and onion.
2 Season with sugar, oyster sauce and soy sauce. Add the shredded ginger and sliced chillies. Mix well and serve, garnish with spring onions.

Tip

Other kinds of mushrooms such as pin mushrooms, straw mushrooms and shiitake mushrooms can be used instead of the ear-mushrooms, used in this recipe.

Serves : 2 persons

Steps

1 Slice the pork fillet thinly.
2 Stir-fry garlic until golden.
3 Add the pork and fry until cooked.
4 Season and mix in the remaining ingredients.

Moo Tod Kra - tiam Prik - thai

(Pepper-Garlic Pork)

Ingredients

300 g. pork fillet, thinly sliced
2 tablespoons soy sauce
1 teaspoon granulated sugar
1/4 teaspoon salt
1/2 teaspoon ground pepper
1 tablespoon oyster sauce
2 tablespoons fried garlic
vegetable oil for deep-frying
carrots blanched or other vegetables

Preparation

1 Marinate pork with soy sauce, salt, pepper, oyster sauce and sugar. Let stand in refrigerator for about 20 - 30 minutes.
2 Heat vegetable oil until hot, fry the pork until cooked.
3 Arrange on a plate, garnish with boiled carrots or other vegetables. Pour sauce over the pork and sprinkle with fried garlic.

Ingredients for Sauce

3 tablespoons oyster sauce
1 tablespoon chopped garlic
1 teaspoon granulated sugar
2 teaspoons soy sauce
3 tablespoons stock, chicken
1 1/2 tablespoons vegetable oil

Preparation

Heat oil until hot and stir-fry garlic until golden. Add all the seasonings and stock. Bring to a boil, spoon over the fried pork and blanched vegetables which have been previously arranged on the plate.

Serves : 2 persons

Steps

1. Slice the pork fillet.
2. Marinate the pork with all the seasonings.
3. Fry the marinated pork until cooked.
4. Make sauce to pour over the fried pork.

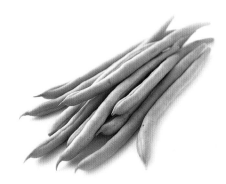

102   104   106

108   110   112

114   116   118

120   122   124

126

Clear Soup (Kaeng Jued)

Clear soup is made by boiling meat and vegetables in a large quantity of liquid and preferably consumed hot. Basic soup stocks are made from boiling meat bones with vegetables and then strain to get a clear stock. A simple method for making soup is to bring soup stock to a boil, then add meat and vegetables Season as desired, while fried garlic and pepper can be sprinkled on clear soup before serving to enhance its aromatic flavour.

Curries (Kaeng Phed)

The main ingredients used are liquid and curry paste. There are 2 basic kinds of curries, namely, those using clear soup stock such as Spicy Clear Red Curry or *Kaeng Pha* and Hot and Sour Vegetable Curry or *Kaeng Som* and those using a coconut milk base as an ingredient such as the Green Curry or *Kaeng Keow Wan* and other thick curries. The names are often derived from the paste used. For example, when green curry paste is used, such curry is called *Kaeng Keow Wan* or Green Curry. Where red curry paste is used, the curry is called *Kaeng Phed*. The main flavours are hot and salty, with some sweetness coming from coconut milk or added sugar. In preparing, curry paste is stir fried with coconut milk. Meat along with vegetables that take longer to cook can be added once the coconut milk begins to bubble with traces of oil surfacing. Season as desired then add the easily cooked vegetables such as basil and kaffir lime leaves.

Hot and Sour Soup (Tom Yum)

This is usually made by using clear stock as a base similar to making other clear soup, although coconut milk or milk is also sometimes used. *Tom Yum* has a strong and tangy flavour, similar to the taste of Thai salads. Sour, salty and hot tastes are prevalent in this kind of soup. The tartness in *Tom Yum* comes from lime or tamarind concentrate. Fish sauce or table salt adds to the saltiness while the spiciness is from the crushed bird chillies, fried dried red chillies or even from mixing the roasted chilli paste into the soup.

Tom Yum is usually seasoned with each individual bowl prior to serving in order to retain the fresh taste. Similar to Thai salads, the additional seasonings are added according to individual preferences.

Boiling (Thoon)

This is the method of cooking by boiling until tender. This used to be a very lengthy process but nowadays, by using a pressure cooker, time can be considerably reduced.

Kaeng Keow – wan Kai

(Green Chicken Curry)

Ingredients

300 g. chicken, cut into pieces
½ cup carrots, cut into pieces
½ young shoot of coconut tree, cut into pieces
½ cup eggplants, pieces
½ cup string beans, cut into pieces
¼ cup green curry paste (page 31)
3 cups coconut milk
2 tablespoons vegetable oil
¼ cup fish sauce
2 teaspoons granulated sugar
3 kaffir lime leaves, shredded
4 - 5 green and red spur chillies, sliced diagonally
½ cup sweet basil leaves

Preparation

1 Stir-fry the green curry paste with vegetable oil until aromatic. Add the chicken and continue frying until cooked, add sugar and fish sauce, stir in the coconut milk.
2 Put in carrots, young coconut shoot, string beans and eggplants, bring to a boil.
3 Then, chillies, kaffir lime and sweet basil leaves are added last. Remove from heat and serve with steaming rice or Chinese rice-flour vermicelli.

Tip

Pea eggplants can be used as well as round eggplants.

Serves : 4 persons

Steps

1. Stir-fry the curry with oil until aromatic.
2. Add chicken and continue to fry until cooked, add seasonings.
3. Put the fried chicken into the pot of coconut milk.
4. Add all vegetables and boil until cooked.

Tom - klong Pla Krob

(Hot and Sour Dried Smoked Fish Soup)

Ingredients

5 dried smoked Whisker sheat fishes or dried smoke salmon
4 cloves shallots, crushed
6 thin pieces of galangal, crushed
2 sticks lemongrass, cut into pieces and crushed
2 - 3 kaffir lime leaves, shredded
5 bird chillies, crushed
3 cups water
4 tablespoons tamarind concentrate
3 - 4 tablespoons fish sauce
5 dried roasted red bird chillies

Preparation

1 Grilled the dried smoked fishes until aromatic. Remove the bones and set the flesh aside.
2 Bring water to a boil. Put in shallots, galangal, lemongrass and kaffir lime leaves. When boiling, add smoked fishes, crushed fresh bird chillies, tamarind concentrate and fish sauce. Add the roasted dried red bird chillies just before serving.

Tip

Grilling the dried smoked fish before making the soup will make it more aromatic.

Serves : 3 - 4 persons

Steps

1 Grill the dried smoked fish until aromatic.
2 Remove the bone and set the flesh aside.
3 Bring the water with galangal, lemongrass, kaffir lime leaves and shallots to a boil.
4 Add the fish and boil until tender, add bird chillies and seasonings.

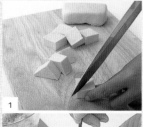

Kaeng Jud Tao - hoo Sod - sai

(Stuffed Bean Curd in Clear Soup)

Ingredients

3 white stuffed bean curds	
250 g. chopped prawns	
1 tablespoon coriander roots	
1 tablespoon garlic	
½ teaspoon white peppercorns	
½ teaspoon corn flour	
3 tablespoons soy sauce	
1 tablespoon fish sauce	
¼ teaspoon salt	
4 cups stock, chicken	
1 cup cabbage, shredded	
¼ cup carrots, diced	
1 spring onions, cut into pieces	
1 coriander, leaves only	

Preparation

1 Cut the bean curds into triangular pieces and remove a little flesh from the middle of the triangles.
2 Pound coriander roots, garlic and peppercorns into a smooth paste.
3 Mix the paste with minced prawns and then add corn flour, fish sauce and salt. Stuff the mixture into the prepared triangular bean curds.
4 Bring the soup stock to a boil. Season with soy sauce to the desired flavour. Put in the stuffed bean curds, cabbage and carrots. When the vegetables are cooked, add spring onions. Ladle into a soup bowl and sprinkle with fried garlic and coriander leaves.

Serves : 3 - 4 persons

Steps

1 Cut the bean curds into bite-sized pieces. Remove part of the flesh from the middle.
2 Mix the minced prawns with the garlic paste.
3 Fill the middle of the bean curds with about 2 teaspoons of the seasoned prawns.
4 Boil the stuffed bean curds in the soup stock until cooked.

Pa - nang Pla Salmon

(Salmon Panang Curry)

Ingredients

2 Salmon steaks

3 tablespoons fish sauce

1 tablespoon palm sugar

2 teaspoons tamarind concentrate

2 cups coconut milk

2 tablespoons vegetable oil

1/4 cup panage curry paste (page 32)

1/2 cup sweet basil leaves

4 - 5 kaffir lime leaves, shredded

1 each green and red spur chillies, sliced into strips

Preparation

1 Heat the vegetable oil, stir-fry the curry paste until aromatic. Add coconut milk and bring to a boil.

2 Season with fish sauce, sugar and tamarind concentrate. Bring to a boil, when the mixture is well blended, add in the Salmon steaks. Continue to boil until cooked. Add kaffir lime leaves. Remove from heat and put in basil leaves.

3 Garnish with the strips of green and red chillies and serve.

Serves : 2 persons

Steps

1 Stir-fry the curry paste in oil until aromatic.

2 Add coconut milk and all the seasonings.

3 Put in the Salmon steaks and until cooked.

4 Add kaffir lime and sweet basil leaves. Remove from heat.

Tom – kha Kai

(Spicy Chicken and Galangal Coconut Soup)

Ingredients

200 g.chicken fillets, cut into pieces

2 cups coconut milk

1 cup water

½ cup young galangal, sliced thinly

kaffir lime leaves, shredded

2½ sticks lemongrass, cut into pieces

2 tablespoons fish sauce

2 - 3 tablespoons lime juice

5 - 7 bird chillies, crushed

coriander leaves

Preparation

Bring the coconut milk and water to a boil. Add galangal, lemongrass and kaffir lime leaves. When boiled, put in the chicken and continue boiling until cooked. Season with fish sauce. Remove from heat, add lime juice and chillies. Garnish with coriander leaves and serve.

Serves : 2 persons

Steps

1   Cut the chicken into bite-sized pieces.
2   Boil galangal, lemongrass and kaffir lime leaves in coconut milk and water.
3   Add the chicken and boil until cooked.
4   Put fish sauce, lime juice and chillies in the bottom of a soup bowl, ladle the hot soup on to the seasonings.

Kaeng – som Phak Ruam

(Hot and Sour Mixed Vegetable Soup)

Ingredients

10 - 12 medium sized prawns, peeled and deveined
$\frac{1}{2}$ cup prawns, cooked
1 cup white Chinese cabbage, sliced
1 cup white radish, cut into pieces
1 cup cabbage, cut into pieces
$\frac{1}{2}$ cup string beans, cut into pieces
1 cup cauliflower, cut into pieces
$\frac{1}{4}$ cup hot and sour curry paste (page 30)
4 cups stock, vegetable
$\frac{1}{3}$ cup fish sauce
$\frac{3}{4}$ cup tamarind concentrate
2 tablespoons palm sugar, optional

Preparation

1 Pound the curry paste with the cooked prawns until smooth. Set aside.
2 Bring the stock to a boil. Add the mixed sour curry paste and prawns, cooked. When boiled, put in the prawns, followed by white radish and cauliflower. When cooked, add string beans, cabbage and white Chinese cabbage and continue cooking.
3 Season with fish sauce, palm sugar (optional) and tamarind concentrate. Bring to a boil, remove from heat and serve.

Serves : 4 persons

Steps

1 Pound hot and sour curry paste with cooked prawns until smooth.
2 Mix the paste into the soup stock.
3 Add prawns into the soup.
4 Put in all the vegetables and seasonings.

Kaeng Jud Wun - sen Song - krueng

(Clear Vemicelli Soup)

Ingredients

1 cup minced pork

½ cup minced prawns

½ cup glass vermicelli, soaked and shortened

1 tablespoon coriander roots

1 tablespoon garlic

1 teaspoon white peppercorns

½ cup carrots, cut into pieces

1½ cup Chinese cabbage, sliced

¼ teaspoon salt

2 tablespoons soy sauce

3 cups stock, chicken

3 spring onions, cut into pieces

1 tablespoon crisp fried garlic

Preparation

1 Pound coriander roots, garlic and pepper together into a smooth paste. Add mince pork and prawns with glass vermicelli, season with fish sauce and mix well, then make into round balls.

2 Bring the stock to a boil. Add the pork and prawn balls until cooked. Add carrots and Chinese cabbage. Season with soy sauce, salt and add spring onions, remove from heat and sprinkle with crisp-fried garlic and serve.

Serves : 3 - 4 persons

Steps

1 Pound coriander roots, garlic and pepper into a smooth paste.

2 Add minced prawns, minced pork, glass vermicelli and seasonings. Mix well.

3 Make round balls of the above mixture and drop them into the boiling soup stock.

4 Put in all the vegetables and bring to a boil. When cooked, season and remove from heat.

Kaeng - kua Sup - pa - rod

(Prawn and Pineapple Red Curry)

Ingredients

2 cups pineapple, cut in squares

7 - 8 medium sized prawns, peeled and deveined

100 g. squids, cut diagonally

100g. sea bass or red snapper, cut in squares

2 cups coconut milk

$\frac{1}{4}$ cup red curry paste (page 30)

2 tablespoons vegetable oil

3 tablespoons fish sauce

2 tablespoons palm sugar

2 - 3 kaffir lime leaves, shredded

1 each red and yellow spur chillies, sliced diagonally

Preparation

Stir-fry the curry paste in oil until aromatic. Add prawns, squid and sea bass and season with fish sauce and palm sugar. Pour in coconut milk and bring to a boil, add the pineapple, stirring until well mixed. Garnish with kaffir lime leaves and sliced chillies. Ladle into a bowl and serve.

Serves : 3 - 4 persons

Steps

1 Cut the pineapple.
2 Stir-fry red curry paste with prawns and squid until cooked.
3 Put in seasonings and add coconut milk. Continue frying.
4 Add pineapple, stirring until well mixed.

Tom – som Pla

(Sweet and Sour Spicy Fish Soup)

Ingredients

3 mackeral steaks
¼ cup young ginger, sliced finely into very thin strips
2 cloves shallot
3 - 4 coriander roots
1 lemongrass, sliced finely
½ teaspoon shrimp paste or 2 teaspoons dried shrimp
½ tablespoon ground pepper
¼ cup palm sugar
⅓ cup tamarind concentrate
3 - 4 tablespoons fish sauce
3 cups water or stock, chicken
2 spring onions, cut into pieces
1 sprig coriander (leaves only)

Preparation

1 Pound shallots, coriander roots, lemongrass, shrimp paste or dried shrimps and ground pepper into a fine paste.
2 Bring water or stock to a boil add fish and the pounded paste, followed by sliced ginger.
3 Season with tamarind concentrate, fish sauce and palm sugar. Garnish with pieces of spring onions and coriander leaves.

Tip

Other kinds of fish with firm flesh can be used instead of mackerel.

Serves : 3 - 4 persons

Steps

1 Pound the shallots, coriander roots, lemongrass and shrimp paste or dried shrimp into a fine paste.
2 Mix the paste in water or stock.
3 Add fish and bring to a boil until cooked.
4 Put in sliced young ginger and seasonings.

Kaeng Mus - sa - man Kai

(Chicken Mussaman Curry)

Ingredients

3 chicken thighs	
$\frac{1}{2}$ cup potatoes, cut into squares	
3 tablespoons mussaman curry paste (page 32)	
2 cups coconut milk	
$\frac{1}{4}$ cup roasted peanuts	
2 bay leaves	
3 cardamons	
2 tablespoons vegetable oil	
$\frac{1}{4}$ cup palm sugar	
3-4 tablespoons fish sauce	
$1\frac{1}{2}$ tablespoons tamarind concentrate	

Steps

1 Stir-fry the curry paste in oil until aromatic.
2 Add chicken and continue to fry until partly cooked.
3 Add coconut milk and potatoes. Simmer until the chicken and potatoes are almost cooked.
4 Add seasonings, bay leaves and cadamons.

Preparation

1 Stir-fry the curry paste until aromatic. Add the chicken and continue to fry until partly cooked. Set aside.
2 Put the partly cooked chicken, potatoes, peanuts into a pot of coconut milk. With medium heat, bring to a boil. When the chicken and potatoes are almost cooked, season with sugar, fish sauce and tamarind concentrate. Add bay leaves and cadamons. Simmer until the chicken and potatoes are thoroughly cooked. Remove from heat and serve immediately.

Tip

Beef or pork, cut in chunks, can be used instead of chicken thighs. They should be boiled in coconut milk before adding them to the curry paste to give the more delectable taste to the curry.

Serves : 3 - 4 persons

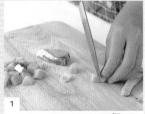

Kaeng – pah Fak – thong Pla in – see

(Spicy Clear Red Curry with Pumpkin and Mackerel)

Ingredients

150 g. Mackerel, cut into squares

½ cup pumpkin, cut into squares

¼ cup spicy curry paste (page 31)

5 cups eggplants, sliced

1 - 2 tablespoons green peppercorns

2 tablespoons vegetable oil

2 tablespoons fish sauce

1 teaspoon granulated sugar

2½ cups water or stock, vegetable

3 kaffir lime leaves, shredded

¾ cup holy basil or red basil leaves

Preparation

1　Stir-fry the curry paste in hot oil until aromatic. Add fish and pumpkin, then pour in half the water or stock. Simmer over medium heat until the pumpkin is cooked.
2　Add the eggplants and green peppercorns. Pour in the remaining water and season with fish sauce and sugar. Bring to a boil, then add kaffir lime and basil leaves. Remove from heat.

Tip

The quartered round eggplants should be soaked in brine to avoid discolouring.

Serves : 2 persons

Steps

1　Cut the fish into squares.
2　Stir-fry the curry paste in hot oil until aromatic.
3　Add fish and pumpkin. Pour in water or stock and simmer until cooked.
4　Add eggplants and green peppercorns. Pour in the remaining water. Season.

Chu - chi Koong

(Stir-Fry Prawn in Red Curry Sauce)

Ingredients

4 - 5 giant freshwater prawns

1½ cups coconut milk

3 - 4 kaffir lime leaves, finely sliced

2½ tablespoons red curry paste (page 30)

2 - 3 tablespoons fish sauce

½ tablespoon palm sugar

2 tablespoons vegetable oil

1 each green, red and yellow spur chillies, sliced finely

Preparation

1 Stir-fry the red curry paste in hot oil until aromatic. Add coconut milk and bring to a boil. Season with fish sauce and sugar.

2 Add the giant freshwater prawns and continue to fry until cooked. Put in the finely sliced kaffir lime leaves and remove from heat. Spoon the prawns on to a plate, pour the sauce over the prawns and serve, garnish with the shredded chillies.

Serves : 2 persons

Steps

1 Extract the coconut milk from shredded coconut flesh.

2 Stir-fry the curry paste in hot oil until aromatic.

3 Add the coconut milk and seasonings.

4 Put in the prawns and continue to fry until cooked.

Tom – yum Koong

(Hot and Sour Prawn Soup)

Ingredients

10 - 15 prawns, peeled and deveined

5 - 6 slices galangal

2 - 3 sticks lemongrass, cut into pieces

3 - 4 kaffir lime leaves, shredded

2½ cups water

¼ cup roasted chilli paste (page 33)

3 tablespoons fish sauce

3 tablespoons lime juice

5 bird chillies, crushed

2 - 3 coriander (leaves only)

Preparation

Put galangal, lemongrass and kaffir lime leaves into water and bring to a boil, add prawns. When cooked, season with roasted chilli paste, fish sauce and lime juice. Garnish with chillies and coriander leaves. Serve imme- diately.

Steps

1 Put galangal, lemongrass and kaffir lime leaves into water and bring to a boil.
2 Add the prawns and continue to boil until cooked.
3 Mix the roasted chilli paste, fish sauce, lime juice and chillies.
4 Pour the soup to the seasoning mixture.

Tip

Milk can be added by reducing water by half and put milk instead to produce a thicker soup.

Serves : 2 persons

130   132   134   136

138   140   142   144

146   148   150   152

154   156   158   160

Salads
(Yum)

The outstanding features of Thai salads are the strong taste and the freshness of the ingredients used. The tastiness includes sourness, saltiness and hotness. As for the sweetness, it is added only to improve the flavour. The tartness can be obtained from lime juice which not only gives the sour taste, but is also especially aromatic. The salty taste comes from fish sauce, the sweet taste from boiling sugar and water to make syrup which is easier when mixing the salad dressing. The hotness in Thai salads derives from crushed bird chillies or pounded roasted dried red chillies. The hot taste helps making the dish more delectable. The taste of the salad dressings depends upon the diners. Chillies can be omitted from the dressings if desired. The sour taste can also be adjusted to taste.

Most of the ingredients used, whether meat or vegetables, are usually cut into small pieces and blanched. Special care must be taken when mixing the salads to avoid bruising the vegetables. Salads must be eaten immediately after the dressings are mixed in.

Spicy Sauces, Chilli Dips
(Krueng Jim, Nam Prik)

Dips in Thai food can be divided into two categories. The first kind has the sour, salty and sweet tastes as found in the chilli dips with vegetables. The main ingredients for chilli dips are different kinds of chillies, roasted shallots and garlic, dried shrimps or grilled fish, shrimp paste, lime juice and fish sauce. The others, with a sweet and sour taste, have coconut milk as a main ingredient. The sourness generally comes from a tamarind concentrate.

These dips are accompanied by vegetables, whether fresh, boiled, egg-coated and fried or stir-fried in oyster sauce, depending on the type of dip.

Lon Koong

(Prawn Coconut Dip)

Ingredients

350 g. minced prawns

100 g. minced pork

2 cups coconut milk

3 tablespoons palm sugar

4 tablespoons tamarind concentrate

4 tablespoons fish sauce

½ cup shallots, finely sliced

1 each green and red spur chillies, cut into pieces

vegetables such as cucumber, white Chinese cabbage and eggplant

Preparation

1 Bring coconut milk to a boil, add prawns and pork. When cooked, add the shallots.
2 Season with tamarind concentrate, fish sauce and palm sugar. Stir until well blended. Put in the chillies and when boiled, remove from heat. Serve with a selection of vegetables.

Tip

Hard white bean curd is added to the dip instead of meat for healthful purpose. Either pork or prawn can be used as preferred.

Steps

1 Bring coconut milk to a boil. Add pork and prawns.
2 Blend in the sliced shallots.
3 Season with tamarind concentrate.
4 Add chillies and stir until well mixed.

Serves : 2 persons

Pla Lui Suan

(Fish in the Garden)

Ingredients

1 medium sized sea bass (about 500 g. in weight)

¼ cup all purpose flour

vegetable oil for deep-frying

Preparation

Clean the fish and wipe dry. Dip in flour, deep-fry in hot oil (medium heat) until golden, drain and put on a plate.

Ingredients for the Sauce

¼ cup garlic, thinly sliced

¼ cup shallots, sliced

3 tablespoons kaffir lime leaves, sliced finely

2 tablespoons chopped coriander leaves

3 tablespoons spring onions, finely sliced

3 sticks lemongrass, sliced finely

3 - 5 bird chillies, sliced finely

½ tablespoon dried red chilli powder (optional)

3 tablespoons fish sauce

4 tablespoons lime juice

2 tablespoons granulated sugar

¼ cup roasted chilli paste (page 33)

fresh vegetables

Preparation

Mix lime juice, sugar, fish sauce and roasted chilli paste together with all the other ingredients and pour over the fried fish. Serve with fresh vegetables.

Serves : 2 persons

Steps

1 Cut diagonally slashes across the fish and deep-fry until golden.
2 Mix lime juice, sugar, fish sauce and roasted chilli paste together.
3 Mix all the ingredients together.
4 Pour the mixture over the fried fish.

Nam – prik Pla – tu – na

(Tuna Dip)

Ingredients

1 can tuna in water
1 tablespoon dried shrimps, pound until fine and fluffy
4 spur chillies
5 cloves shallot, peeled
10 cloves garlic, peeled
2 tablespoons fish sauce
1 tablespoon lime juice
$\frac{1}{2}$ teaspoon granulated sugar
$\frac{1}{4}$ cup boiled water

Preparation

1 Sear garlic, shallot and spur chillies together until cooked. Set aside.
2 Pound all the above ingredients into a smooth paste. Mix in the tuna and season with fish sauce, lime juice and sugar. Taste for the desired flavour. Add water, stir until well blended and sprinkle white dried shrimps. Serve with fresh vegetables.

Serves : 2 persons

Steps

1 Sear spur chillies, shallots and garlic until cooked.
2 Pound the chillies, shallots and garlic into a fine paste.
3 Add tuna and mix well.
4 Season with fish sauce, lime juice and sugar.

Nam – prik Khai Tom

(Boiled Egg Dip)

Ingredients

2 hard boiled eggs

5 - 6 red and green spur chillies

2 tablespoons dried shrimps, coarsely chopped

5 cloves garlic, sliced thinly

2 tablespoons fish sauce

2 tablespoon lime juice

2 teaspoons granulated sugar

Preparation

1 Sear the chillies, peeled and shredded. Set aside.
2 Mix lime juice, fish sauce and sugar together to the desired flavours.
3 Add the shredded seared chillies, followed by dried shrimps and garlic. Pour the mixture over the boiled eggs.

Tip

Bring water to the boil, then put in the eggs. Continue to boil for about 5 minutes. Remove from boiling water and immediately plunge into cold water so that the egg yolks will not be too hard.

Serves : 2 persons

Steps

1 Halve the boiled eggs.
2 Sear the spur chillies.
3 Using a fork, shred the seared chillies.
4 Add dried shrimps, chillies, garlic in the dressing and mix well.

Pla Hed Song - krueng

(Spicy Mushroom Salad)

Ingredients

100 g. white ear mushrooms
50 g. black ear mushrooms
100 g. straw mushrooms
100 g. shiitake mushrooms
100 g. pin mushrooms
150 g. prawns, blanched
4 tablespoons lime juice
3 tablespoons fish sauce
2 tablespoons roasted chilli paste (page 33)
1½ tablespoons granulated sugar
3 tablespoons lemongrass, finely sliced
1 tablespoon kaffir lime leaves, finely sliced
1 tablespoon parsley, finely chopped
¼ cup mint leaves
3 tablespoons sliced shallots
3 tablespoons sliced garlic
5 - 7 red bird chillies, sliced finely
fresh vegetables

Steps

1 Mix lime juice, fish sauce, sugar, roasted chilli paste and bird chillies together.
2 Blanch all mushrooms in boiling water until cooked.
3 Mix the mushrooms with the dressing.
4 Add the remaining ingredients.

Preparation

1 Mix lime juice, fish sauce, sugar, roasted chilli paste and bird chillies together.
2 Bring water to a boil and blanch all the mushrooms until cooked, then drain. Mix all ingredients with the mushrooms. Serve with fresh vegetables.

Serves : 3 - 4 persons

Nam - prik - ong

(Spicy Minced Pork and Tomato Dip)

Ingredients

1½ cups minced pork

1 cup tomatoes, chopped finely

3 tablespoons granulated sugar

¼ cup fish sauce

2 tablespoons vegetable oil

curry paste

spring onions for garnishing

Preparation

1   Stir-fry the curry paste in hot oil until aromatic. Add minced pork and chopped tomatoes, continue cooking.
2   Add with fish sauce and sugar. Spoon into a bowl and sprinkle with chopped spring onions. Serve with fresh vegetables such as cucumbers, white Chinese cabbage, winged beans, string beans and carrots.

Ingredients for Curry Paste

5 dried red bird chillies

5 dried red spur chillies, cut into pieces

3 cloves shallot

6 cloves garlic

1 teaspoon shrimp paste

Preparation

Pound all the ingredients together into a smooth paste. Set aside.

Serves : 3 - 4 persons

Steps

1   Soak the pieces of dried red spur chillies until soft.
2   Pound all the ingredients for curry into a smooth paste.
3   Stir-fry the minced pork and the curry paste until well cooked.
4   Add the chopped tomatoes and seasonings.

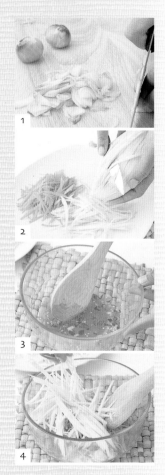

Yum Ma – muang

(Green Mango Salad)

Ingredients

1 cup green mango, shredded

1 cup carrots, shredded

¼ cup shallots, sliced finely

¼ cup dried shrimps, pound until fine and fluffy

4 bird chillies

1 clove garlic, medium size

2 tablespoons lime juice

2 tablespoons fish sauce

2 tablespoons granulated sugar

Preparation

Pound the bird chillies and garlic into a fine paste. Add lime juice, fish sauce and sugar. Mix in the remaining ingredients and serve.

Tip

The dried shrimps can be put in an electric grinder or can be pounded by hand until fluffy.
Apple can be substituted for mango, julienne slice and soak in water with a few drops of lime to prevent turning brown.

Serves : 2 - 3 persons

Steps

1 Sliced shallot cloves finely.
2 Shredded mango and carrots.
3 Mix bird chillies, garlic, lime juice, fish sauce and sugar together.
4 Mix the dressing with all ingredients.

Yum Sam Krob

(Three-of-a-kind Crispy Salad)

Ingredients

1/4	cup crisply fried dried shrimps
1/4	dried smoked whisker sheat fish
1/4	cup crisply fried squid bladders
1/4	cup crisply fried cashew nuts
1/4	cup crispy pork sheets
1/4	cup shredded green mango
1	onion or shallots, sliced into long strips
1/4	cup celery, cut into pieces
1/4	cup lime juice
1/4	cup fish sauce
1	tablespoon granulated sugar
1 - 2	teaspoons bird chillies, crushed
	salad greens, cabbage and string beans

Preparation

1 Mix lime juice, fish sauce, sugar and bird chillies together. Taste to the desired flavours.
2 Add the onion, celery and green mango and mix well together. Then put in the remaining ingredients and serve with the salad greens or cabbage or string beans.

Tip

Break into small pieces and deep-fry 5 ingredients to make crispy.

Serves : 2 - 3 persons

Steps

1 Shredded the green mango.
2 Add the dressing to the sliced vegetables.
3 Put in all the remaining ingredients.
4 Mix well.

Yum Ma - khuea - yao

(Grilled Eggplant Salad)

Ingredients

2 long eggplants or Chinese eggplants
1 hard boiled egg
¼ dried shrimps
3 tablespoons shallots, finely sliced
2 - 3 tablespoons garlic, finely sliced
1 tablespoon fresh bird chillies, finely sliced
3 tablespoons fish sauce
3½ tablespoons lime juice
1 - 2 tablespoons granulated sugar
mint leaves (optional)

Preparation

1 Grill or broil the eggplants until soft. When cooled, peel and cut into pieces. Arrange on a plate and set aside.
2 Mix fish sauce, lime juice, sugar and bird chillies together, add shallots, garlic and mix well.
3 Pour the mixture over the eggplants, dried shrimps and top with boiled egg and mint leaves.

Tip

The boiled egg and dried shrimps can be substituted with boiled shredded chicken or any other kind of meat.

Serves : 2 - 3 persons

Steps

1 Grill or broil long eggplants until soft.
2 Peel the skin.
3 Cut the eggplant in half or ⅔ long.
4 For dressing: mix fish sauce, lime juice, sugar, bird chillies, shallots and garlic together.

Yum Pla Foo

(Fluffy Catfish Salad)

Ingredients

500 g. fried catfish	
$\frac{1}{4}$ cup bread crumbs	
vegetable oil for frying	

Preparation

Flake the fried fillet of fish and mix
with the bread crumbs. Spread out in a tray
and leave about 30 minutes to dry. Then
deep fry in hot oil (medium heat) until
golden. Drain and arrange on a plate.

Ingredients for the Dressing

$\frac{1}{2}$ cup green mangoes, shredded	
$\frac{1}{4}$ cup shallots, sliced thinly	
$\frac{1}{4}$ cup roasted peanuts, crushed	
$\frac{1}{4}$ cup fish sauce	
$\frac{1}{4}$ cup lime juice	
2 tablespoons granulated sugar	
$1\frac{1}{2}$ tablespoons chopped garlic	
2 teaspoons chopped coriander roots	

1 tablespoon fresh bird chillies,
sliced finely

7 fried dried red bird chillies

Preparation

Mix coriander, garlic, shallots and
chillies together. Season with fish sauce,
lime juice and sugar. Pour the dressing
on the fried fish and sprinkle the shredded
green mangoes and crisply fried dried
chillies on top.

Tip

Catfish can be supstituted with fresh tuna or
trout.

Serves : 2 persons

Steps

1 Flake the fish fillet.
2 Mix with bread
   crumbs.
3 Deep-fry the breaded
   fish in hot oil.
4 Mix coriander, garlic,
   shallots and bird
   chillies together with
   the seasonings.

Som – tum Koong Sod

(Spicy Green Papaya Salad with Prawn)

Ingredients

7 - 8 prawns, blanched

1 cup shredded green papaya

½ cup shredded carrots

2 string beans, cut into pieces

5 cherry tomatoes

2 tablespoons dried shrimps

2 tablespoons roasted peanuts, crushed

2 - 4 bird chillies

4 - 5 cloves garlic

2 tablespoons palm sugar

2 - 3 tablespoons fish sauce

1½ tablespoons lime juice

1 tablespoon tamarind concentrate

¼ cup cashew nuts

Preparation

1   Pound garlic, chillies, dried shrimps and peanuts, coarsely. Add string beans, also lightly pounded. Season with lime juice, palm sugar, tamarind concentrate and fish sauce.
2   Add the tomatoes, carrots and papaya and lightly mix together. Mix in the blanched prawns and fried cashew nuts. Dish out and serve with fresh vegetables.

Tip

Horse crabs or salted land crabs can be used instead of prawns. The amount of sugar should be reduced a little to make a better taste.

Serves : 2 persons

Steps

1   Shred the green papaya and carrots.
2   Coarsely pound garlic, chillies, dried shrimps and peanuts.
3   Add string beans, seasonings and tomatoes, mix together.
4   Add the carrots and papaya. Mix well.

Yum Tua - poo

(Winged Bean Salad)

Ingredients

2 cups winged beans, sliced thinly

½ cup boiled pork, sliced

7 - 8 medium sized prawns, peeled and deveined, blanched

½ cup roasted shredded coconut

¼ cup roasted peanuts

¼ cup crispy fried sliced shallots

⅓ cup thick coconut cream, or coconut milk

2 tablespoons roasted chilli paste (page 32)

3 red spur chillies, sliced finely

3 tablespoons fish sauce

3 tablespoons granulated sugar

3 tablespoons lime juice

Preparation

1 Mix sugar, fish sauce, lime juice and roasted chilli paste together.

2 Stir the coconut cream over low heat until thickened. Remove from heat and set aside.

3 Mix winged beans, prawns, pork, peanuts and roasted shredded coconut together with the seasonings. Arrange on a plate and spoon the coconut cream on top. Sprinkle with the shredded spur chillies and crispy fried sliced shallots.

Serves : 4 persons

Steps

1 Heat the coconut cream and set aside for topping.

2 Sliced winged beans thinly.

3 Mix sugar, fish sauce, lime juice and roasted chilli paste.

4 Mix all ingredients with the dressing.

Yum Ruam – mite Ta – lay

(Mixed Seafood Salad)

Ingredients

7 - 10 prawns, peeled and deveined

150 g. squids, sliced diagonally into pieces

150 g. sea bass, cut in squares

100 g. mussels, blanched

½ cup shredded carrots

½ cup onion, thinly sliced

½ cup tomatoes, cut into pieces

½ cup celery, cut into pieces

1 spring onion, sliced finely

2 tablespoons fish sauce

2 tablespoons lime juice

1 tablespoon granulated sugar

5 bird chillies, crushed

fresh vegetables

Preparation

1 Blanch the prawns, squids, sea bass and mussels until cooked. Set aside.
2 Mix fish sauce, lime juice, sugar and chillies together. Add the seafood and the remaining ingredients. Serve over fresh green salad.

Tip

To reduce fishy smell sprinkle fish corn flour let be for 10 - 15 minutes rinse off flour prepare.

Serves : 2 - 3 persons

Steps

1 Cut the squids diagonally.
2 Blanch squids, prawns, mussels and fish until cooked.
3 For dressing mix fish sauce, lime juice, sugar and chillies together.
4 Add fresh green salad and mix together.

Nam - tok Moo / Neeu Nam - tok

(Spicy Grilled Pork or Beef)

Ingredients for Grilled Pork

250 g. pork or beef

½ tablespoon soy sauce

1 teaspoon granulated sugar

¼ teaspoon salt

¼ teaspoon ground pepper

2 tablespoons granulated sugar

2 tablespoons fish sauce

2½ tablespoons lime juice

1 teaspoon dried red chillies

¼ cup parched rice ground coapse

Preparation

Marinate the pork or beef with all ingredients and leave for about 30 minutes. Then grill or sear in a frying pan. Set aside.

Ingredients for the Spicy Pork

200 g. grilled pork or beef, sliced into pieces

5 cloves shallot, finely sliced

3 tablespoons spring onions, finely sliced

3 tablespoons parsley, finely sliced

¼ cup mint leaves

Preparation

1 Thiny slice the grill pork. Set aside.
2 Mix the fish sauce, sugar, lime juice and dried red chillies. Add the grill pork or beef and the remaining ingredients. Mix well and serve with fresh vegetables.

Tip

Use any cut of pork or beef with some fat for flavour.

Serves : 3 - 4 persons

Steps

1 Marinate the pork or beef with the seasonings.
2 Grill the marinated pork / beef or sear on a frying pan.
3 Thinly slice the grill pork.
4 Mix with all ingredients.

Yum Pla Tu – na

(Tuna Salad)

Ingredients

150 g. tuna in brine, drained	
1/4 cup shallots, finely sliced	
1/4 cup carrots, finely sliced	
1/4 cup green mango, finely sliced	
1/4 cup young ginger, finely sliced	
2 tablespoons garlic, finely sliced	
3 tablespoons fish sauce	
3 1/2 tablespoons lime juice	
1 teaspoon granulated sugar	
5 bird chillies, finely sliced	
1/4 cup roasted peanuts	
spring onions and coriander leaves for garnishing	
fresh vegetables	

Preparation

Mix fish sauce, sugar, lime juice and chillies together. Add tuna and the remaining ingredients. Mix well and dish out, garnish with spring onions, coriander leaves and roasted peanuts. Serve with fresh vegetables.

Serves : 2 persons

Steps

1 Slice garlic across thinly.
2 Mix sugar, fish sauce, lime juice and chillies together.
3 Add tuna meat and mix well.
4 Mix the remaining ingredients with the dressing.

Yum Yai

(Thai Great Salad)

Ingredients

250 g. boiled chicken breast, shredded

8 - 10 medium sized prawns, peeled and deveined

100 g. pork liver, boiled and sliced thinly

150 g. pork, boiled and shredded

3 hard boiled eggs, sliced

$\frac{1}{4}$ cup glass vermicelli, soaked in water and blanched

$\frac{1}{2}$ cup ear mushrooms, sliced into strips

$\frac{1}{2}$ cup roasted peanuts, crushed

$\frac{1}{2}$ cup cucumbers, sliced thinly

1 clove onion, sliced

$\frac{1}{4}$ cup pickled garlic, sliced thinly

$\frac{1}{4}$ cup mint leaves

1 celery, cut into pieces

$\frac{1}{2}$ cup lime juice

$\frac{1}{4}$ cup fish sauce

$\frac{1}{4}$ cup granulated sugar

5 red spur chillies, thinly sliced

lettuce leaves

Steps

1 Shred the boiled chicken breast and set aside.
2 Mix fish sauce, lime juice and sugar together.
3 Add all other ingredients pour dressing and mix well.
4 Put in red chilli strips, cucumbers and peanuts.

Preparation

1 Mix fish sauce, lime juice and sugar together. Set aside.
2 Add the chicken, pork, blanched prawns, liver, glass vermicelli, pickled garlic, ear mushrooms onion and celery into pour dressing over. Mix well together.
3 Put in the red chilli strips, cucumbers and roasted peanuts. Mix gently. Garnish with boiled eggs and mint leaves. Serve on a plate lined with lettuce leaves.

Serves : 3 - 4 persons

164

166

168

170

172

174

176

178

180

182

184

186

188

190

192

194

196

198

200

202

Starters, snacks and savories (Ar-Harn Waug)

These are served as between-meal snacks or appetizers. Often eaten before lunch or dinner, the portions served are smaller than the main meal. They can be eaten both as a savory and a sweet. These snacks are usually bite-sized for convenience in serving and consuming. Particular attention to details in the preparation of these savories is required to produce not only tempting but also attractive presentations. Depending on what type of food is being made, these light servings can be steamed, deep fired, or stir-fired.

Desserts and Thai Sweets (Ka-nom Wan)

Desserts and Thai sweets are usually served after the main meal. Each category is classified according to the method of preparation such as steaming, stirring and baking, or by the main ingredients used such as eggs and glutinous or sticky rice. The process of making attractive and delectable sweets is time-consuming and requires considerable attention to details during the complex and delicate Preparation.

Steps

1 Mince the pork.
2 Combine chopped prawns, minced prawns, pork and lard with all the seasonings.
3 Make into flat rounds and roll in bread crumbs.
4 Deep-fry until golden.

Tod – mun Koong Song – krueng

(Fried Prawn Cake)

Ingredients

200 g. prawns, coarsely chopped
300 g. fresh prawns
150 g. minced pork
50 g. pork lard, diced
1 egg
2 tablespoons soy sauce
2 teaspoons granulated sugar
4 tablespoons corn starch
½ teaspoon salt
1 teaspoon sesame oil
2 teaspoons ground pepper
bread crumbs
vegetable oil for deep-frying
ketchup

Preparation

1 Mix prawns, pork and pork lard together until firm. Season with sugar, soy sauce, salt, pepper and sesame oil. Add the corn starch and mix, refrigerate for about 15 minutes to make firm.
2 Remove mixture from refrigerate and make into flat round. Dip in beaten egg and roll in bread crumbs.
3 Deep-fry in hot oil (medium heat) until golden brown. Drain and serve with ketchup.

Tip

Other sweet sauces such as plum sauce can be used instead of tomato ketchup.

Serves : 3 - 4 persons

Kuay - teow Bok

(Flat Rice Flour Noodles with Mixed Vegetable Salad)

Ingredients

300 g. wet rice fresh sheet noodles,
cut into 3 x 3 inch squares

200 g. boiled pork, diced

100 g. dried shrimps, soaked in water

200 g. bean sprouts

½ cup thin omelet, sliced into long strips

½ cup roasted peanuts

½ cup cucumbers, diced

½ cup mint leaves

¾ whole lettuces

Ingredients for the Dressing

1½ tablespoons chopped garlic

1½ tablespoons chopped coriander roots

2 teaspoons chopped bird chillies

3 tablespoons fish sauce

3½ tablespoons lime juice

1 - 2 teaspoons granulated sugar

Preparation

Mix fish sauce, lime juice and sugar together. Taste to the desired flavour. Then add garlic coriander roots and bird chillies and mix well. Set aside and serve with the noodle.

Seving

Place the noodle squares on top of a lettuce leaf. Then put pork, dried shrimps, bean sprouts, shredded egg, roasted peanuts, cucumbers and mint leaves in the middle, add the dressing. This comprise of one mouth full.

Tip

This can be arranged in groups on a platter ready to serve.

Serves : 3 - 4 persons

Steps

1 Cook egg like crepe.
2 Slice the egg into thin strips.
3 Mix all the seasonings for the dressing.
4 Place the noodle square on a lettuce leaves and put top with remaining ingredients.

Steps

1 Shred angle mushrooms into thin strips.
2 Deep-fry until golden and crisp.
3 Stir-fry the garlic, peppercorns and coriander root paste.
4 Mix the crisp mushrooms with the mixture, sprinkle with sesame seeds.

Hed - sa - wan

(Sesame Mushroom)

Ingredients

500 g. angle mushrooms, shredded
1 tablespoon chopped garlic
1 tablespoon chopped coriander roots
1 teaspoon peppercorns
4 tablespoons soy sauce
$\frac{1}{4}$ cup palm sugar
$\frac{1}{4}$ cup white sesame seeds, roasted
2 tablespoons oil for stir-frying
vegetable oil for deep-frying

Preparation

1 Deep-fry the mushrooms until golden and crisp. Drain.
2 Pound coriander roots, garlic and peppercorns together. Stir-fry until aromatic, add soy sauce and palm sugar. Continue cook until well mixed.
3 Add the mushrooms to the mixture, stirring gently. Sprinkle sesame seeds all over. Remove from heat and serve when cooled. This dish can also be kept for many days in a closed container.

Serves : 4 persons

Sa – tay Kai

(Chicken Satay)

Ingredients

500 g. chicken fillets, sliced thinly

1 teaspoon ground coriander

1/2 teaspoon ground cumin

1/2 tablespoon curry powder

1 tablespoon all purpose sauce

1/2 cup sweetened condensed milk

1/4 teaspoon salt

Preparation

Marinate the chicken with all the ingredients and leave for about 30 minutes. Thread the marinated chicken onto skewers and grill until cooked.

Ingredients for Satay Sauce

1/2 cup mussaman curry paste (page 32)

1/4 cup ground peanuts

1/2 tablespoon tamarind concentrate

2 cups coconut milk

1/4 cup palm sugar

3 tablespoons fish sauce

Steps

1 Slice the chicken fillet thin.
2 Marinate the chicken with curry powder, cumin seed powder, all purpose sauce, sweetened condensed milk and salt.
3 Thread the marinated chicken on skewers.
4 Grill or broil the satay until cooked.

Preparation

1 Pound the curry paste and peanuts together. Set aside.
2 Bring coconut milk to a boil until fat surfaces. Add the curry paste, stirring until blended. Add fish sauce, palm sugar and tamarind concentrate. Set aside in a bowl.

Sweet and Sour Cucumber Relish Ingredients

1/2 cup vinegar

2 tablespoons granulated sugar

1 teaspoon salt

1/4 cup water

sliced cucumbers

cloves of shallots, sliced thinly

fresh green and red spur chillies, sliced

Preparation

Bring vinegar, water, sugar and salt to a boil. Set aside to cool. Put cucumbers, sliced shallots and chillies in a serving bowl and pour the syrup over until just covered.

Serves : 4 persons

Peek – kai Pun – kon

(Fried Stuffed Chicken Wing)

Ingredients

8 - 10	chicken upper wings

½ cup cooked crabmeat

½ cup carrots, finely chopped

2 tablespoons chopped garlic

1 tablespoon coriander roots, sliced finely

2 teaspoons peppercorns

2 tablespoons soy sauce

½ teaspoon salt

1 egg

1 cup bread crumbs (for coating)

vegetable oil for deep-frying

ketchup

Preparation

1 Pound coriander roots, garlic and peppercorns to a fine paste. With a pointed knife, remove the skin and discard, then take the flesh and mince finely. Clean the bones. Set aside.
2 Combine the minced chicken, crabmeat, chopped carrots with the pounded paste. Add soy sauce and knead together.
3 Cover the bones with the mixture from 2 and coat in bread crumbs. Deep-fry in hot oil (medium heat) until golden. Drain and serve with ketchup.

Tip

Chicken wings may be steamed to precook before deep-frying.

Serves : 4 persons

Steps

1 Remove the meat from chicken upper wings and mince.
2 Mix minced chicken, crabmeat and carrots with all the seasonings.
3 Roll mixture into ball and place on end of chicken bone like a drumstick.
4 Dip in beaten egg and roll in bread crumbs. Deep-fry until golden.

Khao – thang – na – tang
(Coconut Dip with Crispy Rice Cracker)

Ingredients

$^3/_4$ cup minced pork

$^1/_2$ cup minced prawns

$^1/_4$ cup roasted peanuts, ground

$^1/_2$ tablespoon chopped garlic

$^1/_2$ tablespoon chopped coriander roots

$^1/_4$ teaspoon peppercorns

1 cup coconut milk

2 tablespoons fish sauce

1 tablespoon granulated sugar

$1^1/_2$ tablespoons tamarind concentrate

coriander leaves and shredded chillies for garnishing

dried rice crackers

1 - 2 tablespoons roasted chilli oil

Preparation

1 Pound coriander roots, garlic and peppercorns into a fine paste. Set aside.
2 Bring coconut milk to a boil until the oil surfaces. Add the paste, minced pork, minced prawns and peanuts. Stir to mix and season with fish sauce, sugar and tamarind concentrate. This dip should have salty and sweet flavours. Remove from heat and put a few drops of roasted chilli oil on top. Garnish with coriander leaves and shredded chillies. Serve with deep-frying crispy rice crackers.

Steps

1 Pound coriander roots, garlic and peppercorns together.
2 Mix the paste with coconut milk. Add minced pork and prawns.
3 Add peanuts.
4 Deep-fried dried rice crackers until golden and crispy.

Tip

The rice crackers can be substituted with any kind of thin unseasoned cracker. The rice cracker shown in step 4 in un-cooked rice cracker.

Serves : 2 - 3 persons

Ka – nom – pang Na Koong Chub Nga

(Sesame Prawn Toast)

Ingredients

10 pieces of bread or bagaette, sliced diagonally

10 prawns, peeled and deveined

$\frac{1}{2}$ cup minced prawns

2 tablespoons white sesame seeds

2 eggs white

2 teaspoons chopped garlic

2 teaspoons chopped spring onions

1 tablespoon chopped coriander roots and leaves

2 tablespoons corn starch

1 tablespoon fish sauce

$\frac{1}{2}$ teaspoon ground pepper

vegetable oil for deep-frying

Preparation

1   Put the bread in the oven at 150°C for about 5 minutes. Set aside to cool.
2   Mix minced prawns with garlic, chopped spring onions, coriander, corn starch, fish sauce, pepper and eggs white together. Set aside.
3   Spread the mixture on the toast, top with the whole prawn and sprinkle with white sesame seeds. Deep-fry on medium heat until golden drain and serve with plum sauces.

Serves : 3 - 4 persons

Steps

1   Slice the bread thinly.
2   Mix together the minced prawns, garlic, chopped spring onions, coriander, corn starch, fish sauce, pepper and eggs white.
3   Spread the mixture on top of the bread. Put the whole prawn on top and sprinkle with white sesame seeds.
4   Deep-fry in hot oil until golden.

Ka – nom – pang Na Moo

(Pork Toast)

Ingredients

15 pieces sandwich bread, cut into squares
1 cup minced pork
2 eggs
2 tablespoons corn starch
½ teaspoon salt
2 teaspoons soy sauce
vegetable oil for deep-frying
coriander leaves
red spur chillies, sliced into thin strips

Preparation

1   Put bread into the oven at 150°C or 350°F for about 15 minutes. Set aside to cool.
2   Mix together minced pork, eggs, corn starch, salt and soy sauce. Then spread over the pieces of bread, garnish with coriander leaves and chilli strips.
3   Deep-fry in hot oil (medium heat) until golden. Serve with cucumber relish or sauces.

Ingredients for Cucumber Relish

2 red spur fresh chillies, coarsely ground
¼ cup shallots, sliced thinly
¼ cup water
½ cup vinegar
½ cup granulated sugar
1 teaspoon salt
3 - 4 cucumbers, sliced diagonally

Preparation

1   Bring sugar, salt and vinegar to a boil. Set aside to cool.
2   Mix the syrup with cucumber slices, ground chilli and sliced shallots. Set aside to serve with pork toasts.

Tip

The process baking the bread helps lessen the greasiness when deep-fried.

Serves : 4 persons

Steps

1   Cut bread into bite-sized squares.
2   Mix all the ingredients with minced pork.
3   Spread the pork mixture on top of the bread.
4   Deep-fry in hot oil until golden.

Khao – pode Tod Song – krueng

(Fried Sweet Corn Cake)

Ingredients

1½	cups yellow corn, chopped, or fresh corn
1	cup minced pork
1	egg
1	tablespoon chopped coriander roots
1	tablespoon pounded garlic
1	teaspoon peppercorns
1	tablespoon all purpose flour
1	teaspoon salt
1	teaspoon granulated sugar
	vegetable oil for deep-frying
	chilli sauce or ketchup

Preparation

1 Pound together coriander roots, garlic and peppercorns and set aside.
2 Mix the corn, pork, flour, egg together with the pounded paste.
3 Season with salt and sugar. Mix well, then deep-fry in hot oil (medium heat) until golden. Drain and serve with chilli sauce or ketchup.

Serves : 3 - 4 persons

Steps

1 Pound coriander roots, garlic and peppercorns into a paste.
2 Slice the fresh corn thinly.
3 Mix the corn with all ingredients.
4 Deep fry in hot oil until golden.

Poo – ja
(Deviled Crab)

Ingredients

200 g. minced pork

200 g. minced prawns

200 g. boiled crabmeat

2 eggs

1 tablespoon chopped coriander roots

1 tablespoon chopped garlic

2 teaspoons peppercorns

4 tablespoons soy sauce

2 teaspoons granulated sugar

3 tablespoons spring onions, finely sliced

1 egg for coating

vegetable oil for deep-frying

6 - 8 medium sized crab shells

red spur chillies, sliced into thin strips

Preparation

1 Pound coriander roots, garlic and peppercorns into a fine paste. Set aside.
2 Mix the crabmeat, pork, minced prawns, 2 eggs and spring onion with the above paste. Season with clear soy sauce and sugar. Knead until firm.
3 Fill the crab shells with the mixture and steam for about 20 - 25 minutes until cooked. Set aside to cool. Dip the stuffed crab shells in beaten egg, garnish with strips of red chilli and deep-fry until golden. Drain and serve with plum sauces.

Steps

1 Pound coriander roots, garlic and peppercorns into a fine paste. Set aside.
2 Mix the crabmeat, pork, minced prawns, eggs, spring onion together with the coriander roots, garlic and pepper paste. Season.
3 Fill the crab shells with the seasoned mixture and steam until cooked.
4 Dip the stuffed crab shells in beaten egg and deep-fry until golden.

Tip

Mixture can be made into patties, steamed and deep-fried.

Serves : 3 - 4 persons

Kluay Chuem

(Banana in Syrup)

Ingredients

8 - 10	small bananas (not so ripe)
1½	cups granulated sugar
3	cups water
½	cup coconut milk
½	teaspoon salt

Preparation

1 Heat coconut milk, with salt added, stirring until thicken. Do not boil. Set aside.

2 Bring water and sugar to a boil. Add small bananas and stew in syrup until cooked. Serve with the prepared coconut milk.

Tip

Use baby banana or any kind available.

Serves : 4 persons

Steps

1 Peel bananas.
2 Bring water and sugar to a boil.
3 Add bananas and continue boiling.
4 When the bananas are cooked and golden in colour, remove from the syrup.

Ta – koh Sa – ku

(Tapioca Pudding with Coconut Cream Topping)

Ingredients

½ cup tapioca pearl

¼ cup tapioca flour or corn starch

3 cups water

¼ cup thick juice from pandanus leaves

(bai teoy) or vanilla extract

1½ cups granulated sugar

Preparation

1 Mix tapioca pearl, tapioca flour, water and pandanus juice or vanilla extract together. Stir over heat until cooked. When the mixture thickens, add sugar and continue stirring until sugar is dissolved.

2 Spoon the tapioca mixture into a dish or serving receptacle, topped with the prepared coconut cream.

Ingredients for CoConut Cream Topping

2 cups coconut milk

½ cup rice flour

1 tablespoon granulated sugar

1 teaspoon salt

Preparation

Mix coconut milk, rice flour, salt and sugar together. Stir over low heat until cooked and thickened. Spoon over the pudding.

Serves : 4 persons

Steps

1 Wash the tapioca pearl.

2 Mix the tapioca pearl, tapioca flour, water and pandanus juice or vanilla extract together.

3 Stir tapioca pearl over heat until cooked and thickened. Add sugar.

4 Spoon the pudding mixture into prepared receptacles and top with coconut cream.

Woon - sang - ka - ya

(Coconut Custard Jelly)

Ingredients

2 tablespoons gelatin
3 duck eggs
$\frac{1}{4}$ cup granulated sugar
$1\frac{1}{4}$ cups palm sugar
1 cup coconut milk
3 cups water

Preparation

1 Beat eggs with banana or pandanus leaves, add palm sugar and coconut milk. Mix well and pass through cloth. Set aside.
2 Heat the gelatin and water until dissolved, add sugar and bring to a boil, add pour in the coconut mixture, stirring quickly until boiled. Spoon into the molds.

Tip

- Pandanus and banana leaves for aromatic optional vanilla extract can be substituted.
- Chicken eggs can be used instead of duck eggs.

Serves : 3 - 4 persons

Steps

1 Beat the eggs with banana or pandanus leaves.
2 Add palm sugar and coconut milk.
3 Pass through thin cloth or a sieve.
4 Heat the gelatin and water until dissolved.

Kluay - buad - chee

(Banana in Coconut Milk)

Ingredients

2 - 3 fragrant bananas (not so ripe)

2 cups coconut milk

⅓ cup granulated sugar

1 teaspoon salt

½ cup young coconut flesh, cut into pieces (optional)

3 tablespoons white sesame seeds, roasted

Preparation

1 Boil bananas about 20 minutes until cooked. Peel and cut into bite-sized pieces.
2 Mix coconut milk, sugar and salt together. Stir over heat until the sugar is dissolved. Taste for the desired flavours, and then add the bananas. Continue boiling until the coconut milk is seeped into the bananas. Add young coconut flesh, stirring well.
3 Serve in a bowl, sprinkle sesame seeds on top.

Serves : 4 persons

Steps

1 Boil bananas until cooked.
2 Peel bananas and cut into bite-sized pieces.
3 Boil bananas in coconut milk.
4 Put in young coconut flesh and season with sugar and salt.

Mor – kaeng Puek

(Baked Taro Coconut Custard)

Ingredients

1 cup taro, boiled and mashed	
1½ cups eggs white	
1 cup coconut milk	
1 cup palm sugar	
2 tablespoons rice flour	
fried sliced shallots	
pandanus leaves	

Preparation

1 Beat the eggs with the pandanus leaves for about 5 minutes. Add palm sugar and continue to squeeze until the sugar is dissolved.
2 Mix in the coconut milk strain the through cloth.
3 Add mashed taro and rice flour to the coconut mixture. Pour into a baking dish or tray. Bake in the oven of 200°C (400°F) for 20 - 25 minutes or until golden and cooked. Sprinkle fried sliced shallots on top.

Steps

1 Beat the coconut milk from shredded coconut flesh
2 Beat the eggs with pandanus leaves for 5 minutes.
3 Pass the mixture through a sieve.
4 Add the taro to the mixture, pour into a baking dish or tray.

Tip

Fried sliced shallots are made by slicing the cloves of shallots thinly and deep-fry until golden and crisp. Drain the crisp fried shallots are usually used in cooking some dishes or to sprinkle in over sweets.

Serves : 3 - 4 persons

Ka - nom Fak - thong

(Steamed Pumpkin Pudding)

Ingredients

500 g. cooked pumpkin, mashed

$\frac{1}{2}$ cup shredded coconut

$\frac{3}{4}$ cup coconut milk

1 cup granulated sugar

1 cup rice flour

$\frac{3}{4}$ cup tapioca flour

$\frac{1}{2}$ teaspoon salt

1 cup skinned coconut boiled

Preparation

1 Combine the rice flour and tapioca flour together. Add coconut milk, sugar and shredded coconut. Mix together with salt and pumpkin.

2 Put the mixture into molds and steam for 15 minutes until cooked. Remove from molds sprinkle skinned coconut boiled on top.

Tip

Pumpkin can be diced and mixed with the coconut custard and steamed in bowls or trays. When cooked, cut into pieces and serve.

Serves : 4 persons

Steps

1 Mash cooked pumpkin.

2 Mix rice flour and tapioca flour with coconut milk, sugar and shredded coconut until well mixed.

3 Add pumpkin.

4 Put in molds and steam until cooked.

Woon - ma - prow - on

(Young Coconut Jelly)

Ingredients

1 tablespoon powdered gelatin
1 cup young coconut juice, liquid in coconut
2¼ cups coconut milk
1 teaspoon salt
1 cup granulated sugar
1 cup young coconut flesh

Preparation

Put the powdered gelatin into coconut juice and stir over heat for 5 minutes or until dissolved. Add coconut milk, sugar and salt, continue to boil until well blended. Pour into moulds. When cool, remove from moulds and serve.

Tip

Jelly is more delicious when chilled.
The coconut juice is a beverage department or the liquid in side the coconut can be used.

Serves : 4 persons

Steps

1 Cut the young coconut flesh into strips, set aside.
2 Heat gelatin and young coconut juice until dissolved.
3 Add coconut milk, sugar, salt and boil until well mixed.
4 Put the mixture into the moulds to set.

Sang - ka - ya Fak - thong

(Steamed Whole Pumpkin with Coconut Custard)

Ingredients

5 duck eggs

1 cup thick coconut milk

3/4 cup palm sugar

4 pandanus leaves, optional

2 small pumpkins, remove seeds

Preparation

1 Mix the eggs with palm sugar and beat with pandanus leaves until well mixed. Add coconut milk.
2 Pass through cloth and pour into the pumpkins. From which the seeds have already been removed. Steam (medium heat) about 1 hour or until cooked.

Tip

The custard mixture can be cooked in a dish with the diced pumpkins mixed into custard.

Serves : 4 persons

Steps

1 Beat duck eggs and palm sugar with pandanus leaves until well mixed.
2 Mix in coconut milk.
3 Pass the mixture through cloth.
4 Pour into the pumpkins and steam until cooked.

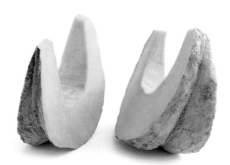

Tub – tim – krob

(Mock Pomegranate Seeds in Coconut Milk Syrup)

Ingredients

500 g. water chestnuts, peeled

2 cups tapioca flour

1 cup red or green syrup or food colouring

Preparation

1 Dice the water chestnuts into small squares and soak in red or green syrup for about 15 minutes. Remove and drain.

2 Toss water chestnuts in tapioca flour, shaking the excess flour off. Then put them into boiling water until cooked (the chestnuts will float above water). Remove from the boiling water and plunge immediately into cold water. Serve in coconut syrup.

Ingredients for Coconut Syrup

1 cup water

2 cups granulated sugar

2 cups coconut milk

Preparation

1 Mix sugar and water together and bring to a boil until the sugar is dissolved. Remove from heat when thickened. Set aside to cool.

2 Heat coconut milk over low heat until boiled but not bubble over. Set aside.

Tip

The mock pomegranate seeds (diced water chestnuts) can be tossed in flour and boiled again to enlarge the size.

Serves : 3 - 4 persons

Steps

1 Soak the diced water chestnuts in different coloured syrups.

2 Drain and toss in tapioca flour.

3 Using a sieve, shake the excess flour off.

4 Boil the chestnuts until float on top. Remove and plunge into cold water.

Bua - loy Song - krueng
(Glutinous Rice Balls in Coconut Milk Mixture)

Ingredients for the Rice Balls

1½	cups glutinous rice flour
¼	cup tapioca flour
½	cup water

Preparation

1 Mix water, a little at a time, with glutinous rice flour and knead until the dough is smooth and firm.
2 Make the dough into small balls about 1 cm. in diameter. Then coat the balls lightly with tapioca flour so that they do not stick together in lumps.
3 Bring water to a boil and put in the rice balls. When they float to the surface, remove and soak in cold water. Drain.

Ingredients for Coconut Milk Mixture

¼	cup coconut cream (the top part of coconut milk)
2	cups coconut milk
¾	cup palm sugar
1	teaspoon salt

Preparation

Mix coconut cream, coconut milk, palm sugar and salt together and pass through a sieve. Bring to a boil and set aside to eat with the glutinous rice balls.

Ingredients for Glutinous Rice Balls in Coconut Milk

½	cup cooked glutinous rice balls
2	tablespoons pumpkin blanched, diced
2	tablespoons taro blanched, diced
1-2	tablespoons sweet corn blanched, grains removed from the cob
½	cup coconut milk mixture

Serving

Put all the above ingredients in a bowl. Add the coconut milk mixture and serve.

Tip

Other boiled cereals such as pearl barleys, mung bean halves or red beans can also be used as desired.
Food colours can be added to the flour to give colours to the rice balls.

Serves : 4 persons

Steps

1 Mix glutinous flour with water and knead into a smooth paste.
2 Make small balls, 1 cm. in diameter.
3 Coat the balls with tapioca flour to avoid sticking together in lumps.
4 Boil the balls in boiling water until float to the surface. Remove from the water and submerge in cold water.

Thai Select Restaurants in Europe

THE POPULARITY OF THAI CUISINE HAS RESULTED IN THE PROLIFERATION OF RESTAURANTS THROUGHOUT EUROPE SERVING AUTHENTIC THAI DISHES SOME OF WHICH ARE LISTED HERE.

AUSTRIA

Vienna

ECHO DER CITY THAI RESTAURANT
Passauerplatz 2, 1010 Vienna, Austria
Tel +43 15338984
Email office@echo-citythai.cc
www.echo-citythai.cc

PINONG THAI RESTAURANT
Seiden Gasse 2, 1070
Vienna, Austria
Tel/Fax +43 15239920

SIAM RESTAURANT
Bosendorferstrasse 2-4,
1010 Vienna, Austria
Tel +43 15053846
Email siam-vienna@gmx.at
www.siam-vienna.at

BHUNG BUI RESTAURANT
Burggasse 44, 1071 Vienna
Tel 01 523 4747
Email office@bhungbui.at
www.bhungbui.at

MUANG THAI RESTAURANT
Wasshubergasse 11,
2700 Wr Neustadt
Tel/Fax 026226921-4
Email thairestaurant@aou.at
www.thairestaurant.at

BELGIUM

Brussels

BLUE ELEPHANT BRUSSELS
1120 Chaussee de Waterloo,
1180 Brussels, Belgium
Tel +32 23744962
Email brussels@blueelephant.com
www.blueelephant.com

MITRA ORIGINAL THAI CUISINE
15 Place Sainte-Catherine,
1000 Brussels, Belgium
Tel +32 22179012
Email mitra.brussels@skynet.be
www.mitrathaicuisine.com

MY-TAI
110 Chaussee de Malines,
1970 Wezembeek Oppem, Belgium
Tel +32 27312726
Email info@my-tai.be
www.my-tai.be

NOI
6 Place Communale,
1630 Linkebeek, Belgium
Tel +32 23806860
Email noi@noi.be
www.noi.be

SUKHOTHAI
135 Avenue D'Auderghem,
1040 Brussels, Belgium
Tel +32 26494366
Email panawat45@hotmail.com
www.restosukhothai.be

Others

SAVEURS DU MONDE
26 Rue Adolphe Sax,
5500 Dinant, Belgium
Tel +32 82222029
Email marcoz12@yahoo.fr
http//home.euphonynet.be/saveurs_du_monde

ZETA (THAI WHITE HOUSE)
34 Eikestraat,2500 Lier, Belgium
Tel +32 32945366
Email zeta@lunch-lounge-dinner.com
www.lunch-lounge-dinner.com

DENMARK

Copenhagen

BAN GAW
Hamtovet 44, 1700 Copenhagen, Denmark
Tel +45 33228438, 33254860
Email bangaw@ofig.dk
www.bangaw.dk

BAN GAW 1
Istedgade1,DK-1650,
Copenhagen V, Denmark
Tel +45 33222620, 33222621
Email bangaw@ofig.dk
www.bangaw.dk

BLUE ELEPHANT
Amager Boulevard 70, Radisson
SAS Scandinavia Hotel, 2300
Copenhagen, Denmark
Tel +45 33965724
Email copenhagen@blueelephant.com
www.blueelephant.dk

THAI THAI TAKEAWAY AND BUFFET
Valdemarsgade 46, 1665
Copenhagen, Denmark
Tel + 45 33230081
www.thai-thai-takeaway.dk

Others

BANGKOK RESTAURANT
Kongensgade 13,
3550 Slangerup, Denmark
Tel +45 47380160
www.bangkokrestaurant.dk

LEMONGRASS THAI CUISINE RESTAURANT
Tovegade 5, 3000 Helsingor,
Tel +45 49251511
Email shepsut@gmail.com

WHITE-ELEPHANT
Klostergade 1,
8000 Arhus C, Denmark
Tel +45 86129499
Email nattaya@white-elephant.dk
www.white-elephant.dk

FINLAND

Jyvaskyla

BANTHAI RAVINTOLA
Kortesuon Katu 26, 40700
Jyvaskyla, Finland
Tel +358 0143100069
Email ravintola@banthai.fi
www.banthai.fi

Naantali

THAI GARDEN RESTAURANT
Naantali Spa Hotel, Matkailijantic
2,221100 Naantali, Finland
Tel +358 244550
Email chefmanit@fastmail.fm
www.naantalispa.fi

FRANCE

Paris

BAAN THAI
13-15 Rue de La Ferronerie
75001 Paris, France
Tel +33 142338525

BAI THONG
47 Rue De Charenton 75012 Paris
Tel +33 0143 475547

BAN SOM TAM
5 rue Reymond Losserand
75014 Paris, France
Tel +33 0143 226572

BANYAN
24 Place Etienne Pernet
75015 Paris, France
Tel +33 0140 600931

BLUE ELEPHANT
43-45 Rue de la Roquette
75011 Paris, France
Tel +33 147004200
Email paris@blueelephant.com
www.blueelephant.com

CHIENG MAI
12 Rue Frederic Sauton
75005 Paris, France
Tel +33 143254545

ERAWAN
76 Rue de la Federation
75015 Paris, France
Tel +33 147835567

KHUN AKORN
8 Avenue de Taillebourg
75011 Paris, France
Tel +33 143562003

KRUA THAI
41 Rue de Montparnasse
75014 Paris, France
Tel +33 143353867

KRUNG THEP
93 Rue Julien Lacroix Paris
75020, France
Tel +33 143668374

European Thai Select Restaurants Healthy & Easy Thai Cooking

KONFUSIUS THAI RESTAURANT
20 Allee de la Mane Jacob 91290
La Norville, France
Tel +33 169269040

LA THAILANDAISE
1 bis Rue de l'Aure 75015
Paris, France
Tel +33 145773678

MAI THAI
24 bis, rue St.Gilles 75015, Paris
Tel +33 0142 721877

PATAYA
29 Rue Etienne Marcel 75001
Paris, France
Tel/Fax +33 142339809

PHETBURI
31 Bd. de Grenelle 75015
Paris, France
Tel/Fax +33 140581488

PHO 27
27 Bd. de la Villette 75010
Paris, France
Tel +33 142102920

RAJAPREUK
18 Rue Mayet 75006, Paris
Tel +33 0145 665157

REUAN THAI
36 Rue de l'Orillon 75011
Paris, France
Tel +33 143551582

SALA THAI
13 Rue des Freres d' Astier
de la Vigerie
75013 Paris, France
Tel +33 145841322

SAWADE
53 Rue Emile Zola 75015
Paris, France
Tel +33 145776890

SIAMIN
19 Rue Bayard 75008, Paris
Tel +33 0147 202370

SUAN THAI
41 Rue ste. Croix bretonnerie
75001, Paris
Tel +33 0142 771020

SUKHOTHAI
12 Rue du Pere Guerin 75013
Paris, France
Tel +33 145815588

TAMARIND
33 Rue Francois Miron 75001,
Paris
Tel +33 0148 873420

THAB THIM SIAM
28 Rue De Moscou 75008
Paris, France
Tel +33 143876256

THIOU
49 Quai d' Orsay 75007
Paris, France
Tel +33 140629650

WASANA
10 Rue Ganneron 75018
Paris, France
Tel/Fax +33 144700854

Others

BANGKOK ROYAL
40 Rue du Sergent Blandan
69001 Lyon, France
Tel +33 478281982

BANYAN
189 Rue de Solferino 59000
Lille, France
Tel +33 320572020

BANN THAI
10 rue Kageneck 67000, Strasbourg
Tel 0388 320839

BANN THAI
22 Boulevard Jean Baptiste Lebas
59777, Lille
Tel 0320 860601

KONFUSIUS THAI RESTAURANT
20 Cour des Lacs 77200, Torcy
Tel 0160 174147

LA TABIE DE SIAM
79 rue de la Monnaie 59000, Lille
Tel 0320 556047

GERMANY

Berlin

CAFE RATANA RESTAURANT
Bundesallee 95, 12161 Berlin,
Germany
Tel +49 3085103039

DAO
Kantstr. 133, 10625 Berlin, Germany
Tel +49 3037591414

EDD'S
Luetzower Str. 81,
10785 Berlin, Germany
Tel +49 302155294

GOOD TIME RESTAURANT
(ZEHLENDORF)
Teltowerdamm 46,
14167 Berlin-Zehlendorf, Germany
Tel +49 3084591852
www.goodtime-berlin.de

MALAGO BAR-RESTAURANT
Krossener Str. 15,
10245 Berlin, Germany
Tel +49 3021238848
Email info@papaya-service.de
www.papaya-service.de

MAO THAI (MEIEROTTOSTR.)
Meierotto Str. 1,
10719 Berlin, Germany
Tel +49 308832823

MAO THAI (WOERTHERSTR.)
Woerther Str. 30,
10405 Berlin, Germany
Tel +49 304419261
Email info@maothai.de
www.maothai.de

PAGODE THAI KITCHEN
Bergmann Str. 88,
10961 Berlin, Germany
Tel +49 306912640
www.pagode-thaifood.de

PAPAYA
Krossener Str. 11,
10245 Berlin, Germany
Tel +49 3029771231
www.papaya-service.de

PAPAYA AM KLEISPARK
Hauptstr. 159, 10827 Berlin, Germany
Tel +49 3081494254
Email info@papaya-service.de
www.papaya-service.de

SALA THAI (FRANKFURTUR ALLEE)
Frankfurter Allee 73 (Plaza),
10247 Berlin, Germany
Tel +49 3042812020
Email sorapong@santiburi.com
www.salathai.de

**SAMRAN THAI IMBIS
& RESTAURANT**
Winterfeldstr. 35,
10781 Berlin, Germany
Tel +49 3021964752
Email samran@hotmail.com

SIDA
Ahornstr. 32, 12163 Berlin, Germany
Tel +49 307923670

THAI BORAN
Friedrichstr. 127,
10117 Berlin, Germany
Tel +49 3056735514

THAI-INSIDE
Dircksenstr. 37, 10178 Berlin, Germany
Tel/Fax +49 3024724371
Email mail@thai-inside.de
www.thai-inside.de

TUANS HUETTE
Dircksenstr. 40,
10178 Berlin, Germany
Tel +49 302836940

VIENGTHAI RESTAURANT
Pank Str. 50,
13357 Berlin, Germany
Tel +49 304653052

Bochum

PATTAKAN-THAI
Brockhauser Str. 42,
44797 Bochum, Germany
Tel +49 2347980176
Email pattakan-thai@t-online.
www.pattakan-thai.com

PRATHUM THAI
Nordring 100,
44787 Bochum, Germany
Tel/Fax +49 2346407174
Email kontakt@prathum-thai.
www.prathum-thai.de

Dusseldorf

BAAN THAI
Berger Str. 28,
40213 Duesseldorf, Germany
Tel +49 211326363

NAKHON THAI
Pempelforter Str. 45,
40211 Dusseldorf, Germany
Tel/Fax +49 2113613870

NOPPAKAO
Bismarck Str. 33-35,
40210 Duesseldorf, Germany
Tel/Fax +49 2118693700

SILA THAI
Bahn Str. 76,
40210 Duesseldorf, Germany
Tel +49 2118604427
www.sila-thai.com

Frankfurt

BANGKOK
Sandweg 17,
60316 Frankfurt/M., Germany
Tel +49 69491360

KOH SAMUI
Grosse Friedberger Str. 32,
60313 Frankfurt, Germany
Tel +49 69292828

KRUA THAI RESTAURANT
Jordan Str. 10, 60486
Frankfurt-Bockenheim, Germany
Tel +49 69774105
Email kruathai92@yahoo.de

PHANWADEE
THAI RESTAURANT
Dreieichstr. 7,
60594 Frankfurt, Germany
Tel/Fax +49 6996248888

PIMAI THAI
RESTAURANT & COCKTAIL
Schwarzwaldstr. 46,
60528 Frankfurt, Germany
Tel +49 6967739465

RAMA V
Vilbeler Str. 32,
60313 Frankfurt, Germany
Tel +49 6921996488

SASIWAN RESTAURANT
Eschersheimer Land str. 65,
60322 Frankfurt, Germany
Tel +49 695971030

SUVADEE THAI RESTAURANT
Steinweg 7,
60313 Frankfurt, Germany
Tel +49 69285477
www.suvadee.de

Hanover
ORIGINAL THAI HAUS
Vahrenwalder Str. 18,
30165 Hanover, Germany
Tel +49 5113742474

THAI ORCHIDE
Konig Str. 7,
30175 Hanover, Germany
Tel +49 511344367

Hamburg
BAAN THAI
Gaensemarkt 50,
20354 Hamburg, Germany
Tel +49 40340441
Email nitipongvik@hotmail.com
www.baanthai.de

SALA THAI
Brandsende 6,
20095 Hamburg, Germany
Tel +49 40335009
Email sorapong@santiburi.com
www.salathai.de

Cologne
SIAM (KOELN)
Grosse Neugasse 42,
50667 Cologne, Germany
Tel +49 2212579782

SIAM THAI RESTAURANT
AmBollwerk 15,
5066 Cologne, Germany
Tel +49 2212580602

SUKHOTHAI
Luxemburger Str. 181,
50939 Cologne, Germany
Tel +49 2219411049

VIMAN THAI RESTAURANT
Luxemburger Str. 181,
50939 Cologne, Germany
Tel +49 2214210671

Stuttgart
SAWADI THAI RESTAURANT
Rotebuhlstr. 50,
70178 Stuttgart, Germany
Tel +49 711626232
Email info@sawadi.de
www.sawadi.de

SHABA THAI
Neckarstr. 246,
70190 Stuttgart, Germany
Tel/Fax +49 7112845670
Email shaba_restaurant@yahoo.de
www.shaba-thai-restaurant.de

THAI PALAST
Haussmannstr. 5,
70188 Stuttgart, Germany
Tel/Fax +49 7112364042
Email post@thai-palast.de
www.thai-palast.de

TIFFANY THAISTYLE
Schulstr. 104,
70173 Stuttgart, Germany
Tel +49 7112202762

Wiesbaden
ERAWAN THAI LOCAL
Taunusstr. 59,
65183 Wiesbaden, Germany
Tel +49 6118904933
Email purkpong@t-online.de
www.erawan-wiesbaden.de

PHUKET
Emse 65195 Wiesbaden, Germany
Tel +49 61140907970
www.phuket-wiesbaden.de

Others
AHARN-THAI
Kaiserstr. 36,
66121 Saarbruecken, Germany
Tel +49 6818910899
Email aharn-thai@gmx.info
www.aharn-thai.de

BANGKOK (KONSTANZ)
Braunegger Str. 47, 78462
Konstanz, Germany
Tel +49 753115589
Email
webmaster@bangkokkontanz.de
www. bangkok-kontanz.de

BUUNTRIK
BGM-Smidt-Str. 31,
28195 Bremen, Germany
Tel +49 42118785
Email buuntrik@web.de

CHADA THAI RESTAURANT
Haupt Str. 22,
79364 Malterdingen, Germany
Tel +49 76447305
Email info@chadathai.de
www.chadathai.de

CHIANG MAI (GOETTINGEN)
Nikolausberger Weg 27, 37073
Goettingen, Germany
Tel/Fax +49 5515085803

CHIANG MAI (SCHWAEB. GMUEND)
Josept-Haydn Str. 21, 73525
Schwaeb. Gmuend, Germany
Tel +49 7171182080
www.chiangmairestaurant.de

CHOPRAYA RIVER
Bieberer Str. 260,
63071 Offenbach, Germany
Tel +49 69854366

DOISUTHEP
Markt Str. 16,
31188 Holle, Germany
Tel/Fax +49 50622758

DUANG DAO
Stuhlinger Str. 34,
79106 Freiburg, Germany
Tel +49 7618814881
Email tuibochum@aol.com

NAKORN THAI (KASSEL)
Wilhelmshoeher Allee 40-42,
34119 Kassel, Germany
Tel/Fax +49 561104928
Email kassel2n@hotmail.com
www.nakornthai-restaurant.de

NAKHONSAWAN
Kieler Str. 31,
24594 Hohenwestedt, Germany
Tel +49 4871761878
Email raesch-phamorn@grnx.de

RIM WANG
Eckenerstr. 1,
76185 Karlsruhe, Germany
Tel +49 721697776

SABAI SABAI THAI CUISINE
& COCKTAILS
Hauptstr. 72, 65812 Bad Soden
am Taunus, Germany
Tel +49 61965237272
Email pomion23@yahoo.de

SIAM (BALINGEN-ENDINGEN)
Schoemberger Str. 41, 72336
Balingen-Endingen, Germany
Tel +49 7433383480

SUKHO-THAI
Bochumer Str. 15,
45549 Sprockhoevel, Germany
Tel +49 2324702009
www.sukhothai-online.de

THAIRAMA RESTAURANT
Muhlstr. 28,
67659 Kaiserslautern, Germany
Tel +49 63174340

VILLA THAI
Hugstetterstr. 2,
79224 Umkirch, Germany
Tel +49 766593760

IRELAND

Dublin
BAAN THAI
16 Merrion Road,
Ballsbridge, Dublin 4, Ireland
Tel +353 16608833

DIEP LE SHAKER
55 Pembroke Lane,
Dublin 2, Ireland
Tel +353 16611829
www.diep.net

Carlow
WEEPING THAIGER
Quinn House, Mill Lane,
Carlow, Ireland
Tel +353 599137000

ITALY

Brescia
RHUAN THAI RESTAURANT
Via Indipendenza 40/c, 25123,
S. Eufemia, Brescia, Italy
Tel/Fax +39 030361477

THAI GARDEN RESTAURANT
Via Brescia 15 (SS45bis), 25021
Bagnolo Mella, Brescia, Italy
Tel/Fax +39 030622241

Milan
SPICE SETTECUPOLE THAI
RESTAURANT
Via Ippolito Nievo 33,
20145 Milan, Italy
Tel/Fax +39 02341290
Email info@spicerestaurants.com
www.spicerestaurants.com

LUXEMBOURG

Luxembourg

THAI CELADON
1 Rue du Nord,
L-2229, Luxembourg
Tel +35 2474934
Email resthai@pt.lu
www.thai.lu

THAILAND
72 Ave Gaston Diderich,
L-1420 Luxembourg
Tel +35 2442776
Email resthai@pt.lu
www.thai.lu

NETHERLANDS

Amsterdam

BAAN THAI RESTAURANT
Amstelveenseweg 83,
1075 VW Amsterdam,
Netherlands
Tel +31 206756632
Email leen@immerzeel.nl

BIRD THAI RESTAURANT
Zeedijk 72-74, 1012 BA.
Amsterdam, Netherlands
Tel +31 206201442
Email mertens@zonnet.nl
www.thai-bird.nl

BUSABA AFHAALCENTRUM
Amstelveenaseweg 155-bg,
1075 XA, Amsterdam, Netherlands
Tel +31 206738241
Email welkom@busaba.nl
www.busaba.nl

KRUA THAI RESTAURANT
Staalstraat 90A,
1012 TZ, Amsterdam, Netherlands
Tel/Fax +31 206200623
Email info@kruathai.nl
www.kruathai.nl

KRUA THAI CLASSIC RESTAURANT
Staalstraat 22,
1011 JM, Amsterdam, Netherlands
Tel +31 206229533
Email info@kruathai.nl
www.kruathai.nl

ME NAAM NAAN
Koningsstraat 29,
1011 ET Amsterdam, Netherlands
Tel +31 204233344
Email menaamnaan@xs4all.nl
www.menaamnaan.nl

NA SIAM
Kerkstraat 332, 1431 JA
Amsterdam, Netherlands
Tel +31 204210505
Email b.j.shcooneveldt@wxs.nl

PATHUM THAI RESTAURANT
Willemsstraat 16,
1015 JD, Amsterdam, Netherlands
Tel +31 206244936
Email M.de.Kreij@zap.A2000.nl
www.dinnersite.nl/amsterdam

RAAN PHAD THAI
Klovenierburgwal 18,
1012 CT, Amsterdam, Netherlands
Tel +31 204200665

SONG KWAE
Klovenierburgwal 14A,
1012 CT, Amsterdam, Netherlands
Tel +31 206242568
Email songkwae@xs4all.nl
www.songkwae.nl

THAI DEUM THAIS RESTAURANT
Ceintuurbaan 210,
1072 GD Amsterdamn, Netherlands
Tel/Fax +31 203790705
Email info@thaideum.com
www.thaideum.com

TOP THAI RESTAURANT
Herenstraat 28,
1015 CB Amsterdam, Netherlands
Tel +31 206381415
Email kirtsiri@planet.nl
www.topthai.nl

WHITE ELEPHANT THAI RESTAURANT
Van Woustraat 3,
1074 AA Amsterdam, Netherlands
Tel +31 206795556
Email info@whiteelephant.nl
www.whiteelephant.nl

Den Haag

CHIENGMAI
Denneweg 120,
2514 CL, Den Haag, Netherlands
Tel/Fax +31 703643545

THAI RESTAURANT PHUKET
Schokkerweg 35,
2583 BH, Den Haag, Netherlands
Tel/Fax +31 703063888
Email restaurant_phuket@planet.nl

RAKANG THAI
Beeklaan 344,
2562 BG, Den Haag, Netherlands
Tel +31 703630765
www.rakangthai.nl

RAMAKIEN
Laan Van Meerdervoort 542C,
542C BL, Den Haag, Netherlands
Tel +31 703562352
Email info@ramakien.nl

RUEN THAI RESTAURANT
Nobelstraat 19,
2513 BC, Den Haag, Netherlands
Tel +31 703652255
Email ruenthai@planet.nl
www.ruenthai.nl

SONG PHI NONG THAI RESTAURANT
Wagenstraat 177,
2512 AW Den Haag, Netherlands
Tel +31 703615096
Email reserveer@song-phi-nong.nl
www.song-phi-nong.nl

SUKSIRI
Calileistraat 160,
2564 TL Den Haag, Netherlands
Tel +31 703562139

TOEK TOEK THAIS EETHUISJE
Douzastraat 85A,
2581 RW Den Haag, Netherlands
Tel +31 703063386
Email info@toektoek.nl
www.toektoek.nl

THE PINK ELEPHANT
Wilgstraat 34,
2565 ME Den Haag, Netherlands
Tel +31 703625716
www.thepinkelephant.nl

WARUNEE THAIS EETCAFE
Laan van Meerdervoort 37A,
2517 AD Den Haag, Netherlands
Tel +31 704271225
Email info@warunee.nl
www.warunee.nl

Rotterdam

NOK NOI RESTAURANT
Straatweg 112, 3051BL Rotterdam,
Netherlands
Tel +31 102188024

SIRIPORN THAIS RESTAURANT
Pannekpekstraat 16A,
3011 LG, Rotterdam, Netherlands
Tel +31 104128565

Others

ERAWAN THAI RESTAURANT
Schagchelstraat 13,
2011 HW Haarlem, Netherlands
Tel/Fax +31 235342923
Email erawan@worldonline.nl
www.erawan.nl

LAI THAI
Muntelstraat 12, 5211 PV DEN
BOSCH, Netherlands
Tel +31 736122178
Email laithai@hetnet.nl

SALA THAI
Rijnkade 65,
6811 HC Arnhem, Netherlands
Tel +31 264460848
Email salathai@xs4all.nl
www.salathai.nl

THAI JASMINE AUTHENTIEK THAIS RESTAURANT
Schuuitendiep 78,
9711 RG Groningen, Netherlands
Tel/Fax +31 503123416
Email info@thaijasmine.nl
www.thaijasmine.nl

THAI TIP EETHUIS & AFHAAL
Nieuweburen 95,
8911 EZ Leeuwarden, Netherlands
Tel +31 582162498
Email info@thaitip.nl
www.thaitip.nl

THAIS RESTAURANT SABAI-SABAI
Nooreinde 27,
2311 CB Leiden, Netherlands
Tel +31 715131914
Email info@sabai-sabai.nl
www.sabai-sabai.nl

THAIS RESTAURANT WASANA DEE
Leusderweg 58,
3817 KB Amersfoort, Netherlands
Tel/Fax +31 334655307
Email kiefta@xs4all.nl
www.thaiwasana.nl

THAIS RESTAURANT BAI YOK
Diezerpoortenplas 3,
8011 VV Zwolle, Netherlands
Tel +31 384229882
Email info@baiyok.nl
www.baiyok.nl

JASMINE THAI CUISINE
Molenstraat 136,
5014 NG Tilburg, Netherlands
Tel +31 135810766
Email jasminethaicuisine@yahoo.com
www.jasminethai.nl

SUKHOTHAI ROYAL THAI CUISINE
Tongersestraat 54,
6211 LP Maastricht, Netherlands
Tel +43 3217946
Email sukhothai@home.nl
www.sukhothai.nl

BANGKOK CITY THAI RESTAURANT
Lange Tien Deweg 57,
2801 KG Gouda, Netherlands
Tel +31 182551333
Email bangkok-city@zonnet.nl
www.bangkok-city.nl

NORWAY

Oslo

CHIANG MAI THAI RESTAURANT
Peder Claussonns Gate 4,
0165 Oslo, Norway
Tel/Fax +47 22206209

NAM FAH THAI RESTAURANT
Prinsens Gate 18,
0152 Oslo, Norway
Tel 22 38 2990
Email info@nam-fah.com
www.nam-fah.com

RICEBOWL RESTAURANT THAI CAFE
Youngsgata 4, 0181 Oslo, Norway
Tel +47 22412006
Email ricebowlthai@yahoo.no
www.ricebowl.no

THAI BANGKOK RESTAURANT
Gronlandsleiret 27,
0190 Oslo, Norway
Tel +47 22177003

PORTUGAL

Lisbon

BANTHAI
Rua Fradesso da Silveira,
n 2, Loja 9 Alcantara-Rio,
Alcantara, Lisbon, Portugal
Tel +351 231621184
Email
banthai_restaurante@yahoo.com
www.restaurantebanthai.com

Others

SAWASDEE
Beco Esconso, 11 R/C-2750,
Cascais, Portugal
Tel +351 214847967
Email nop60999@mail.telepac.pt

SUPATRA
Rua General Amilcar Mota 2500-
209 Caldas Da Rainha, Portugal
Tel/Fax +351 262842920

RUSSIA

Moscow

BAAN THAI
Bolshaya Dorogomilovskaya Street,
BLD 11, Moscow, Russia
Tel +7 4952400597
Email baanthai@mail.ru
www.baanthai.ru

BLUE ELEPHANT
Novinsky Boulevard,
31 Moscow, Russia
Tel +7 4955807756
Email moscow@blueelephant.com
www.blueelephant.com

SPAIN

Balearic Islands

BANYAN PALACE
Avda. San Agustin, 73-75 ,
07820 San Antonio (Ibiza), Spain
Tel/Fax +34 971347735
Email banyan-palace@telefonic.net
www.banyan-palace.com

ROYAL SIAM
Camilo Jose Cela, 10,
07014 Palma De Mallorca, Spain
Tel +34 971221605
Email chonprapa@wanadoo.es

Barcelona

THAI GARDENS BARCELONA
Diputacion, 273,
08007 Barcelona, Spain
Tel +34 934879898
Email thai-gardens@hotmail.com
www.thai-gardens.com

THAI SABAI SABAI
Gran Via De Les Corts Catalanas,
674, 08010 Barcelona, Spain
Tel +34 933015365
Email info@sabaisabaibcn.com

Madrid

OAM THONG
Corazon De Maria, 7,
28002 Madrid, Spain
Tel +34 915151049
Email oamthong@oamthong-
spain.com
www.oamthong-spain.com

SILK & SPICE
Avda. Olimpica, 9, 28100
Alcobendas (Madrid), Spain
Tel +34 916620315
Email grupotao@grupotao.com
www.groupsilkandspice.com

THAIDY
C/JORGE JUAN, 54,
28001, Madrid, Spain
Tel/Fax +34 915757897
Email restaurantethaidy@yahoo.es
www.thaidy.es

THAI GARDENS
Jorge Juan, 5, 28001 Madrid, Spain
Tel +34 915778884
Email thai-gardens@hotmail.com
www.thai-gardens.com

Others

THAI GALLERY
Guadalmina Baja, 40-8, 29660 San
Pedro Alcantara (Marbella), Spain
Tel +34 952818392
Email cpz@gmx.net

THE ORIENTAL – HOTEL BOTANICO
Richard Yeoward, 1, 38400 Puerto
Dela Cruz (Tenerife), Spain
Tel +34 922381400
Email
hotelbotanico@hotelbotanico.com
www.hotelbotanico.com

SWEDEN

Stockholm

AMAZING THAI RESTAURANT
Vastgotagatan 2-4, 11827
Stockholm, Sweden
Tel/Fax +46 86150499
Email amazingthai@amazingthai.se
www.amazingthai.se

PHI PHI RESTAURANT
Birgar Jartsgatan 121,
11356 Stockholm, Sweden
Tel +46 86120301
www.phiphi-island.nu

SABAI SABAI
Kammakargatan 44,
11160 Stockholm, Sweden
Tel +46 87900913
www.sabai.se

Others

AMAZING THAI RESTAURANT 2
Salagatan 20, 75320 Uppsala,
Sweden
Tel +46 18106999
Email tob@amazingthai.se
www.amazingthai.se

THAI FAST FOOD
Drottinggatan 55,
60232 Norrkoping, Sweden
Tel +46 11121237
www.thaifastfood.se

AGNES RESTAURANT
Borganas v.28, 784 33 Borlange
Sweden
Tel 024310342

SWITZERLAND

Basel

JEFFERY'S THAI RESTAURANT
Riehenring 77,
CH-4058 Basel, Switzerland
Tel +41 616813070
Email jefferys@tiscali.ch

KRONE KITTIPON'S FINEST THAI CUISINE
Haup Str. 127,
CH-4102 Binningen, Switzerland
Tel +41 614212042
Email mail@kittipon-
thairestaurant.ch
www.kittipon-thairestaurant.ch

SUKHOTHAI RESTAURANT
Bachletten Str. 19,
CH-4054 Basel, Switzerland
Tel +41 612832020
Email vena@tele2.ch

THAI-FAMILY RESTAURANT
Drahtzug Str. 32 (Ecke Hammer
Str.), CH-4057 Basel, Switzerland
Tel/Fax +41 616814045
Email hr.mathys@gmx.ch
www.thaifamily-restaurant.ch

UNITED KINGDOM

Greater London

ADDIE THAI CAFÉ
121 Earl's Court Road, London,
SW5 9RL, UK
Tel +44 (0)207 2592620

ALLSO THAI RESTAURANT
15 Empire Parade, Empire Way,
Wembley, Middlesex, HA9 0RQ, UK
Tel +44 (0)208 7954242

ANNA'S THAI RESTAURANT
1078 1st Floor, Whitgift Centre,
Croydon, CR0 1UX, UK
Tel +44 (0)208 6816601

BLUE ELEPHANT
3-6 Fulham Broadway,
London, SW6 1AA, UK
Tel +44 (0)207 3856595
www.blueelephant.com/london

CELADON
239 Elgin Avenue, Maida Vale,
London, W9 1NJ, UK
Tel +44 (0)207 3288883

CHIANG MAI THAI RESTAURANT
48 Frith Street, London,
W1D 4SF, UK
Tel +44 (0)207 4377444

CRAZY BEAR
26-28 Whitfield Street,
London, W1T 2RG, UK
Tel +44 (0)207 6310088
www.crazybeargroup.co.uk

CHAOPRAYA EAT-THAI
22 St. Christopher's Place,
London, W1U 1NP, UK
Tel +44 (0)207 4860777
Webstie www.eat-thai.net

ESARN KHEAW
314 Uxbridge Road, Shepherds
Bush, London, W12 7LJ, UK
Tel +44 (0)208 7438930
www.esarnkheaw.com

FAT BOY'S
10A, Edensor Road, Chiswick,
London, W4 2RG, UK
Tel +44 (0)208 9948089

FAT BOY'S
33 Heaven Green, Ealing,
London, W5 2NX, UK
Tel +44 (0)208 9985868

HILLTRIBE RESTAURANT
18 Red Lion Street, Richmond,
London, TW9 1RW, UK
Tel +44 (0)208 3329977

JASMINE
16 Goldhawk Road, Shepherds
Bush, London, W12 8DH, UK
Tel +44 (0)208 7437886

KUM LUANG
326-328 Creek Road,
London, SE10 9 SW, UK
Tel +44 (0)208 2934011

KWAN THAI
Unit 1, Hays Galleria, Tooley St.,
London Bridge City, London,
SE1 2HD, UK
Tel +44 (0)207 4037373

LOTUS THAI RESTAURANT
80 Cleveland Street,
London, W1T 6NE, UK
Tel +44 (0)207 5807213

MAI THAI
75 The Broadway, Wimbledon,
London, SW19 1QE, UK
Tel +44 (0)208 5428834

MANGO TREE
46 Grosvenor Place, Belgravia,
London, SW1X 7EQ, UK
Tel +44 (0)207 823888
www.mangotree.org.uk

NAHLING THAI RESTAURANT
106 High Road, East Finchley,
London, N2 9EB, UK
Tel +44 (0)208 8838688

NAHM
5-6 Halkin Street, London,
SW1X 7DJ, UK
Tel +44 (0)207 3331234

NIPA
1st Floor, Royal Lancaster Hotel,
Lancaster Terrace, London,
W2 2TY, UK
Tel +44 (0)207 5516039

PATARA FINE THAI CUISINE
(KENSINGTON)
181 Fulham Road,
London, SW3 6JN, UK
Tel +44 (0)207 3515692

PATARA FINE THAI CUISINE
(KNIGHTSBRIDGE)
9 Beauchamp Place,
London, SW3 1NQ, UK
Tel +44 (0)207 5818820

PATARA FINE THAI CUISINE
(OXFORD CIRCUS)
3&7 Maddox Street,
London, W1S 2QB, UK
Tel +44 (0)207 4996008

PATARA FINE THAI CUISINE
(SOHO)
15 Greek Street,
London, W1D 4DP, UK
Tel +44 (0)207 4371071

PETCH SAYAM
682 High Road, Leytonstone,
London, E11 3AA, UK
Tel +44 (0)208 5566821
www.petchsayamthairestaurant.co.uk

PU'S BRASSERIE
10 Gate Street, Holborn,
London, WC2A 3HP, UK
Tel +44 (0)207 4042126

SOHO THAI
27-28 St. Annes Court,
London, W1F 0BE, UK
Tel +44 (0)207 2872000

SOHPITA THAI CUISINE
431 Upper Richmond Road West,
East Sheen, London, SW14 7PJ, UK
Tel +44 (0)208 8783588

SOM TAM HOUSE
131 Askew Road, Shepherds Bush,
London, W12 9AU, UK
Tel +44 (0)208 7499030
www.somtamhouse.co.uk

SUGAR HUT GROUP
374 North End Road,
London, SW6 9LY, UK
Tel +44 (0)207 3868950
www.sugarhutfulham.com

SUKHO THAI CUISINE
855 Fulham Road,
London, SW6 5HJ, UK
Tel +44 (0)207 3717600

SUK SARAN THAI
29 Wimbledon Hill Road,
London, SW19 7NE
Tel +44 (0)208 9479199

TALAD THAI
320 Upper Richmond Road,
Putney, London, SW15 6TL, UK
Tel +44 (0)208 7898084

TAMNAG THAI
50-54 Westow Hill, Crystal Palace,
London, SE19 1RX, UK
Tel +44 (0)208 7615959

TAWANA
3 Westborne Grove,
London, W2 4UA, UK
Tel +44 (0)207 2293785
www.tawana.co.uk

THAI EXPRESS
24 Chancery Lane,
London, WC2A ILS, UK
Tel +44 (0)207 8310823
Email info@thaiexpress.me.uk
www.thaiexpress.me.uk

THAI PAVILION
78 Kennington Road,
London, SE11 6NL, UK
Tel +44 (0)207 5826333
www.thaipavilion.com

THAI PEPPER
115 Finchley Road, Swiss Cottage,
London, NW3 6HY, UK
Tel +44 (0)207 7228470

THAI POT
1 Bedfordbury, Covent Garden,
London, WC2N 4BP, UK
Tel +44 (0)207 379 580

THAI SQUARE
347-349 Upper Street,
London, N1 0PD, UK
Tel +44 (0)207 7042000
www.thaisq.com

THAI SQUARE
136-138 Minories, London,
EC3N 1NU, UK
Tel +44 (0)207 6801111
www.thaisq.com

THAI SQUARE
19 Exhibition Road, South
Kensington, London, SW7 2HE, UK
Tel +44 (0)207 5848359
www.thaisq.com

THAI SQUARE
1-7 Great Street, Thomas Apostle,
London, EC4V 2BH, UK
Tel +44 (0)207 3290001
www.thaisq.com

THAI SQUARE
2-4 Lower Richmond Road,
London, SW15 1LB, UK
Tel +44 (0)208 7801811
www.thaisq.com

THAI SQUARE
148 Strand, London, WC2R 1JA, UK
Tel +44 (0)2074970904
www.thaisq.com

THAI SQUARE
21-24 Cockspur Street, Trafalgar
Square, London, SW1Y 5BN, UK
Tel +44 (0)207 8394000
www.thaisq.com

THAI THO
20 High Street, Wimbledon,
London, SW19 5DX, UK
Tel +44 (0)208 9461542

THAI UPON THAMES
346 Richmond Road,
East Twickenham, Middlesex,
TW1 2DU, UK
Tel +44 (0)208 8926808

YUM YUM
183-187 Stoke Newington,
High Street, London, N16 0LH, UK
Tel +44 (0)207 2546751
www.yumyum.co.uk

Others
ART OF SIAM
2A-3A Kings Walk, King Street,
Reading, RG1 2HG, UK
Tel +44 (0)118 9512600

BANTHAI
19 Alexandria Drive, Lytham,
St. Annes on Sea, Lancashire,
FY8 1JF, UK
Tel +44 (0)1253 720382
www.banthai.co.uk

MAI THAI @ HOBBS PAVILION
Park Terrace, Hobbs Pavilion,
Cambridge, CB1 1JH, UK
Tel +44 (0)1223 367480

MENU THAI RESTAURANT
345 Fleet Road, Hampshire,
GU51 3NT, UK
Tel +44 (0)1252 621790

SALA THAI
10 Kenwyn Street, Truro,
Cornwall, TR1 3DJ, UK
Tel +44 (0)1872 272363

SIAM HARBOURSIDE
129 Hotwell Road, Clifton,
Avon Bristol, BS8 4RU, UK
Tel +44 (0)1173 306476

SUKHOTHAI RESTAURANT
302-304 Holdenhurst Road,
Bournemouth, BH8 8AY, UK
Tel +44 (0)1202 304305

TASTE OF THAI
117-119 Southgate Street,
Gloucester, GL1 1UT, UK
Tel +44 (0)1452 520894

THAI ELEPHANT
10 Theatre St., Warwick,
CV34 4DP, UK
Tel +44 (0)1926 492044
www.thaigroup.co.uk

THAI HOUSE
3-5 Guildford Crescent, Churchill
Way, Cardiff, CF10 2HJ, UK
Tel +44 (0)2920 387404
www.thaihouse.biz

THAI TAI
22 High Street, Brackley,
Northamptonshire, NN13 7DS, UK
Tel +44 (0)1280 840348
www.thaitai.co.uk

THAILAND NO 1
80-81 Bailgate, Lincoln,
Lincolnshire, LN1 3AR, UK
Tel +44 (0)1522 537000

THE KING AND I
2 Ship Street, Brighton, BN1 1AD, UK
Tel +44 (0)1273 773390

THE SUGAR HUT
4 Opie Street, Norwich,
Norfolk, NR1 3DN, UK
Tel +44 (0)1603 766755

THE THAI HOUSE
6-7 Pegler Way, Crawley,
West Sussex, RH11 7AG, UK
Tel +44 (0)1293 533005

WILAWAN THAI RESTAURANT
9 Baker Street, Stirling,
Stirlingshire, FK8 1BJ, UK
Tel +44 (0)1786 464838

YOD SIAM
Unit 2, 27 Villa Street, Beeston,
Nottingham, NG9 2NY, UK
Tel +44 (0)1159 258217

Buckinghamshire
THAI SQUARE
29 Thames Street, Windsor,
Berkshire, SL4 1PR, UK
Tel +44 (0)1753 868900
Buckinghamshire

EAT THAI (BUCKINGHAM)
14-15 Easton Street, High
Wycombe, Buckinghamshire,
HP11 1NT, UK
Tel +44 (0)1494 532888
www.eat-thai.net

**THE BLUE ORCHID THAI
RESTAURANT & BAR**
The Square, Aspley Guise,
Milton Keynes, Buckinghamshire,
MK17 8DF, UK
Tel +44 (0)1908 282877

**THE BLUE ORCHID THAI
RESTAURANT & BAR**
102-104 Sycamore Road,
Amersham, Buckinghamshire,
HP6 5EN, UK
Tel +44 (0)1494 432245

SIAM BORAAN
18 Church End, Newton Longville,
Milton Keynes, Buckinghamshire,
MK17 0AG, UK
Tel +44 (0)1908 373522

Cheshire
CHILLI-BANANA, WILMSLOW
The Kings Arms Hotel, Alderly
Road, Wilmslow, Cheshire,
SK9 1PZ, UK
Tel +44 (0)1625 539100
www.chillibanana.co.uk

CHILLI-BANANA (MACLESFIELD)
The Merchants House, 59 Buxton
Road, Macclesfield, SK10 1JX, UK
Tel +44 (0)1625 422332
www.chillibanana.co.uk

CHILLI CLUB
Thirlmere Lodge Rectory Lane,
Lymm, WA13 0AQ
Tel +44 (0)1925 757545

CHILLI CLUB
12 Ashley Road, Altrincham,
Cheshire, WA14 2DW
Tel +44 (0)1619 269197

Derbyshire
THAI BORAN
52 Green Lane, Derby,
Derbyshire, DE1 1RP, UK
Tel +44 (0)1332 343933

SIMPLY THAI
2-3 Cavendish Circus, Buxton,
Derbyshire, SK17 6AT, UK
Tel +44 (0)1298 24471

Durham
NUMJAI
19 Milburngate Centre, Durham
City, Durham, DH1 4SL, UK
Tel +44 (0)1913 862020
www.numjai.co.uk

**STAR OF SIAM,
HIGHFIELD HOTEL**
Durham Road, East Rainton,
DH5 9QT, UK
Tel +44 (0)1915 848745

East Sussex
THAI MARINA
13 The Waterfront, Eastbourne,
East Sussex, BN23 5UZ, UK
Tel +44 (0)1323 470414

Edinburgh
CHIANG MAI
15 Dalry Road, Haymarket,
Edinburgh, EH11 2BQ, UK
Tel +44 (0)1313 132797

DUSIT RESTAURANT
49A Thistle Street, Edinburgh,
Midlothian, EH2 1DY, UK
Tel +44 (0)1312 206846

MUANG THAI
97 Hanover Street, Edinburgh,
Midlothian EH2 1DJ, UK
Tel +44 (0)1312 206119

**SIAM THANI THAI
RESTAURANT**
14 Broughton Street,
Edinburgh, EH1 3RH, UK
Tel +44 (0)1314 772724

Essex
SUGAR HUT VILLAGE
93-95 High Street, Brentwood,
Essex, CM14 1RR, UK
Tel +44 (0)1277 200885
www.sugarhutvillage.com

**SANGDAO THAI
RESTAURANT**
14-16 Hill Street, Saffron Walden,
Essex CB10 1JD, UK
Tel +44 (0)1799 506016

THE NEW THAI LIGHT
33 High Street, Halstead,
Essex CO9 2AA, UK
Tel +44 (0)1787 477577

THAI NAVA RESTAURANT
104 Hamlet Court, Westcliff
on Sea, Essex, SS0 7LP, UK
Tel +44 (0)170 2391171

Greater Manchester
PHETPAILIN
46 George Street,
Manchester, M1 4HF, UK
Tel +44 (0)161 2286500

ROYAL ORCHID
36 Charlotte Street,
Manchester, M1 4FD, UK
Tel +44 (0)161 2365183
www.royalorchid.co.uk

THE THAI LOUNGE
14 Radcliffe New Road,
Manchester, M45 7GY, UK
Tel +44 (0)161 7668822

Herefordshire
AROON RAI THAI RESTAURANT
60 Widemarsh Street, Hereford,
Herefordshire, HR4 9HG, UK
Tel +44 (0)1432 279971

**THE OLD SATANG
THAI RESTAURANT**
48 High Street, Bromyard,
Herefordshire, HR7 4AE, UK
Tel +44 (0)1885 483227

Hertfordshire
THAI COTTAGE
149 High Street, Berkhamsted,
Hertfordshire, HP4 3HH, UK
Tel +44 (0)1442 870808
www.thaicottage.com

**THE BLUE ORCHID
THAI RESTAURANT & BAR**
378 High Street, Berkhamsted,
Hertfordshire, HP4 1HU, UK
Tel +44 (0)1442 875557

**THE BLUE ORCHID
THAI RESTAURANT & BAR**
22 The Wynd, Letchworth,
Hertfordshire, SG6 3EN, UK
Tel +44 (0)1462 480066

THE BLUE ORCHID
THAI RESTAURANT & BAR
80 High Street, Harpenden,
Hertfordshire AL5 2SP, UK
Tel +44 (0)1582 461282

Kent
BANGKOK HOUSE
13 Church Street, St. Pauls
Canterbury, Kent, CT1 1NH, UK
Tel +44 (0)1227 471141

PAD THAI
15 High Street, West Malling,
Kent, ME19 6QH, UK
Tel +44 (0)1732 870000

SURIN
30 Harbour Street, Ramsgate,
Kent, CT 11 8HA, UK
Tel/Fax +44 (0)1843 592001
Email info@surinrestaurant.co.uk
www.surinrestaurant.co.uk

Leicestershire
SIAM CORNER
118 London Road, Leicester,
Leicestershire, LE2 0QS, UK
Tel +44 (0)1162 544856

THAI RAINBOW
84-86 Market Street, Ashby-De-La-
Zouch, Leicestershire, LE65 1AP, UK
Tel +44 (0)1530 560404

Somerset
BLUE OCEAN THAI
RESTAURANT
134 High Street, Avon,
Weston-super-Mare, BS23 1HP, UK
Tel +44 (0)1934 429800

MAI THAI
6 Pierrepont Street, Avon,
Bath, BA1 1LB, UK
Tel +44 (0)1225 445557

Staffordshire
ART OF SIAM
30 High Street, Newcastle Under-
Lyme, Staffordshire, ST5 1QL, UK
Tel +44 (0)1782 629664

Suffolk
BAIPO
63 Upper Orwell Street,
Ipswich, Suffolk, IP4 1HP, UK
Tel +44 (0)1473 218402
www.baipo.co.uk

SANGDAO THAI RESTAURANT
160 High Street, Newmarket,
Suffolk, CB8 9AQ, UK
Tel +44 (0)1638 660646

SINGTONG NEEYOM
THAI RESTAURANT
37 Thoroughfare, Halesworth,
Suffolk, IP19 8LE, UK
Tel +44 (0)1986 873737

Surrey
MAE PING
16-18 South End, Croydon,
Surrey, CR0 1DN, UK
Tel +44 (0)208 7600278

MAX'S THAI
2 South Parade, Stafford Road,
Wallington, Surrey, SE6 9AJ, UK
Tel +44 (0)208 6479488

MONTIEN
214 Sandycombe Road,
Kew Gardens, Richmond,
Surrey TW9 2EQ, UK
Tel +44 (0)208 9488487

RUMWONG
16-20 London Road,
Guildford, Surrey GU1 2AF, UK
Tel +44 (0)1483 536092
www.rumwong.co.uk

SIAM FOOD GALLERY
95-97 High Street, Esher,
Surrey, KT10 9QE, UK
Tel +44 (0)1372 477139

SIR & MADAM THAI
RESTAURANT
37 Station Approach,
West Byfleet, Surrey, KT14 6NF, UK
Tel +44 (0)1932 353297

THAI TERRACE
7th Floor, Castle Car Park,
Sydenham Road, Guildford,
Surrey, GU1 3RT, UK
Tel +44 (0)1483 503350

THAISMILES (WEYBRIDGE)
57 Queen Road, Weybridge,
Surrey, KT13 9UQ, UK
Tel +44 (0)1932 857577

West Midlands
KINNAREE THAI RESTAURANT
22 Waterfront Walk,
Birmingham, B1 1SN, UK
Tel +44 (0)121 6656568

THAI EDGE
7 Oozells Square, Brindley Place,
Birmingham, B1 2HS, UK
Tel +44 (0)121 6433993

THAI ORCHID
7 Bennett's Hill, Birmingham, B2 5ST, UK
Tel +44 (0)121 2121000
www.thaigroup.co.uk

THAI VILLAGE I
1594-1596 High Street,
Knowle, Solihull, West Midlands,
B93 0LF, UK
Tel +44 (0)1564 771595
www.thaivillage.co.uk

Yorkshire
CHAOPHRAYA
THAI RESTAURANT
20A First Floor, Blayds Court
Swinegate, Leeds, LS1 4AG, UK
Tel +44 (0)1132 449339

RIM NAM
Wharfal Building, New Road,
Hebden Bridge, West Yorkshire,
HX7 8AD
Tel +44 (0)1422 846888

SALA THAI
13-17 Shaw Lane, Oakbank,
Leeds, LS6 4DH, UK
Tel +44 (0)1132 788400

THAI @ THE TRAVELLERS
20 Main Road, Homesfield,
Dronfield, Sheffield, S18 7WT, UK
Tel +44 (0)1142 890446

TUMNUK THAI
5 Clare Road, Halifax,
West Yorkshire, HX1 2HX, UK
Tel +44 (0)1422 352500